D1617267

Hermann Simon

Beat the Crisis: 33 Quick Solutions for Your Company

 Springer

Hermann Simon
Simon-Kucher & Partners
Haydnstr. 36
53115 Bonn
Germany
hermann.simon@simon-kucher.com

ISBN 978-1-4419-0822-3   e-ISBN 978-1-4419-0823-0
DOI 10.1007/978-1-4419-0823-0

Library of Congress Control Number: 2009932783

Printed on acid free paper

Foreword

The idea for this book came from my wife Cecilia. After having given presentations on the current crisis to managers all over the world, she asked me one Sunday morning in the summer of 2009, "Why don't you write a book about the crisis?" If I decided to take her advice, one thing was immediately clear to me: it would have to be done very quickly. Within one week I had the contract settled with my publisher and a project team assembled at Simon-Kucher & Partners that would support me. A total of one month and eight days had passed between finishing the first chapter and delivering the completed manuscript. As I wrote, the publishing team prepared the production process, the market introduction and the cover design – an unusual application of "simultaneous engineering" in the publishing world.

"Quick solutions" is the key phrase of the book. By this, I mean solutions that can be implemented quickly and that generate quick results. The unexpectedness and magnitude of the crisis has put companies that do not react fast and decisively in great danger. The importance of responding quickly to the crisis cannot be emphasized enough. The many quick solutions offered in this book show that there are various ways and means of beating the crisis. Resignation is certainly not one of them. Despite the urgency, however, companies must absolutely avoid making fatal mistakes. A wrong step might be forgiven in good times, but in the crisis it can result in a company going under. The severity of the crisis demands that you understand its causes, diagnose your specific situation carefully, implement decisively and monitor closely. This book provides practical support for all these aspects.

For the post-war generation, to which I belong, this crisis poses a totally new challenge. In our entire lives, we have been fortunate to experience peace, growth, and prosperity. The last great depression took place before our time. We are now called upon to mobilize all our strengths to fight this secular crisis. This fight must not be limited to firing people and lowering prices. No, we must become active on the sales and revenue fronts if we are to contain the damage and ensure that our companies survive. The purpose of this book is to offer effective solutions to companies, entrepreneurs, managers and employees on how to beat the crisis. The 33 quick solutions won't rid the world of the crisis, but if implemented, they will definitely contribute to containing the damage.

The crisis has been and will continue to be a big challenge for companies all over the world. While positive signals appear on the horizon and give reason for optimism, we must remain proactive and alert. Above all, we must continue our fight against the repercussions of the crisis and for the recovery. The sooner we come back to a path of sustainable growth, the better for our company and our economy.

As an old Asian proverb says: "When the storm comes some build walls, others build windmills." This book is for the companies who build windmills and thus will come of the crisis stronger than those who build walls.

Hermann Simon

Cambridge, MA and Bonn, Germany

Contents

Chapter 4: Quick Solutions for Changing Customer Needs

Chapter 1

Diagnosing the Crisis

In this first chapter the current crisis will be analyzed. Our goal is to give practical advice for managers and companies on how to fight and beat the crisis. Therefore we will focus on concrete issues related to everyday business matters. This book is very different from most other works in that it is not primarily concerned with the macroeconomic aspects of the crisis.

It's a Sales Crisis, Not a Cost Crisis

The current crisis, which started in 2007 and worsened in subsequent years, is a sales and revenue crisis, not a cost crisis. Sales volumes and revenues have dropped to a shocking extent in the ensuing period. In many markets customers are simply refusing to buy. The reason is not that their purchasing power has suddenly evaporated or that prices and costs are too high. Nor is the competition from low-wage countries or an unfavorable dollar exchange rate the main problem, which has been the case in former crises. Indeed, many factors such as declining prices for oil and raw materials have actually induced some relief on the cost and price front. The reason that both private and business customers are refusing to buy is that the fear of the future has them hoarding their money. "Cash is king" is true for companies and consumers alike. In contrast to earlier recessions, consumers' savings rates have gone up.[1] Consumers are not using their savings to make up for lower incomes. One motive for hoarding cash is to make up for losses in their investment portfolios. The more serious the crisis, the more pronounced these tendencies are becoming.

H. Simon, *Beat the Crisis: 33 Quick Solutions for Your Company*,
DOI 10.1007/978-1-4419-0823-0_1, © Hermann Simon 2010

How should companies respond to a crisis of this kind? One aspect is clear in any kind of recession: Everything needs to be done to reduce costs. Most companies have exercised a remarkable cost discipline in recent years. As one CEO expressed it, "We only hired an additional second employee when we needed a third one." There has been immense progress with regard to automation, and costs of many products are a lot lower today than they used to be. This is not only reflected in the ever-sinking prices of consumer electronics. Today, you get a lot more value per dollar when you buy a car than ten years ago. Even sectors such as the food industry had to respond to the pressures of discounters like Wal-Mart in the U.S. or Aldi in Europe to bring down costs.[2] As a consequence, the potential for cost reduction is markedly lower today than it used to be.

If revenues drop by 20, 30, or 40% companies face the challenge of survival itself. In such an extreme situation cost reductions alone will not suffice. No company will manage to lower costs by such drastic percentages within a short period of time. Moreover, in a first step, rationalization usually causes additional costs. Money is saved only after the measures have been implemented and some time has passed. Amortization periods for cost-cutting measures often last months if not years. If the current downturn is a sales and revenue crisis, it has to be fought on the sales and revenue front – with all means available to a company. Many companies have realized this. In a Simon-Kucher study comprising 2,600 industrial companies, 72% of the respondents said that they were going to combat the crisis not only on the cost side but also on the market front.[3]

Even more than in good times, profit and liquidity are imperative. Liquidity must be ensured at all times. According to the late Peter Drucker, profit is the cost of survival. Profit is defined as price times sales volume minus costs. Thus, there are only three profit drivers: price, sales volume, and costs. These fundamental relations are very simple and lead to the inevitable conclusion that all three profit drivers have to be mobilized in this crisis. It is not enough to use only one of the profit drivers, for example, only lowering costs, only changing prices, or only promoting sales. What is needed is a comprehensive program of quick solutions that can be easily implemented and have a fast and strong impact. This book provides such solutions and all three profit drivers will be dealt with. Costs are the topic of Chapter 3. Since there is no doubt about the necessity of action here and literature in this field exists already in abundance, this chapter is rather short. Our emphasis lies on the revenue side.

In Chapters 4–7, a total of 33 quick solutions will be presented including responses to changing customer needs, solutions for the salesforce, solutions for managing offers and prices, and solutions for services. The implementation of these quick solutions will be dealt with in Chapter 8. All quick solutions are practical and will be illustrated by concrete cases.

In view of the magnitude of the downturn it is unrealistic for most companies to defend revenues, sales and profit on the levels of the past boom years. More often the struggle will be against dramatic drops in revenues and profits that threaten a company's existence. If the market demand drops by 40% and a company can achieve a reduction in revenues of "only" 20% this is a huge success. Or if the competitors' prices go down by 20% a company that defends its own price level at –10% can be very proud.

Apart from the quick solutions that make up the core of the book we will discuss longer-term outcomes of the crisis in Chapter 9. This chapter is of a more speculative nature because no one can accurately predict what is going to happen. A characteristic of this crisis is that even finance ministers, central bank presidents, top bankers or leading economists don't fully understand the complexities. Although this does not keep some from making precise forecasts, an increasing number of experts have started to admit that they are at a loss themselves. Economics Nobel Prize laureate Gary Becker, professor at the University of Chicago, responded to a question on the crisis' further development, "Nobody knows. I certainly don't know." More and more experts use metaphors like "a wall of fog" when they speak of the crisis.[4] One insight from this crisis is that it seems highly doubtful that modern economists understand the global economy in all its complexity. In their new book, *Chaotics*,[5] Philip Kotler and John Caslione advise, "Don't trust economists who say they know."

What Are Causes and Effects of the Crisis?

The burst of the American subprime bubble in the summer of 2007 is usually seen as the beginning of the crisis.[6] There can be no doubt that the subprime shock had a trigger function. The deeper causes, however, go back much further and are found in the U.S. monetary policies with the removal of the gold standard by President Richard

Nixon in 1971. Since then, every financial crisis in the U.S. has been fought with the implementation of low interest rates and an expansion of the money supply.[7]

Eventually the long-term effects of these policies had to surface. Initially, the subprime shockwave spread slowly. Such time lags are typical for economic processes. When Lehmann Brothers collapsed on September 15, 2008, it became clear that this would be a crisis of unusual dimensions and unknown duration. Today, it appears naïve that people questioned whether the crisis would spread from the financial sector to the industrial sector or whether it would affect emerging countries. In sectoral and regional terms the economy is always a system of communicating pipes within which strong disruptions can never remain isolated. This applies to the interrelations between the finance and the industrial sector as well as to B2C and B2B markets[8] and to global interdependencies. By 2009, the crisis had definitely reached the economy on a broad scale. And it developed with a force and a swiftness nobody had anticipated. The sudden steepness of the fall had just as strong an effect on the sentiment of business people and the public at large as the extent of the collapse. Figure 1.1 illustrates the combination of steep ascent and steep decline. Similar curves can be found for other regions and other sectors. The steep fall is an almost universal

Fig. 1.1: Steep ascent, steep fall

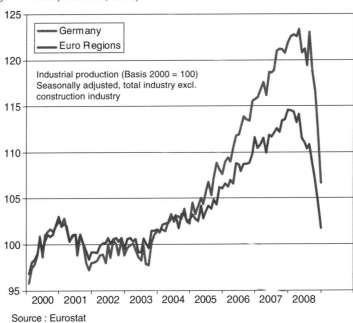

Source : Eurostat

pattern, at least in the industries affected by the crisis. Within six months the progress of the last years was erased. Managers often repeated similar comments such as, "I have never experienced a similar downturn. It hit us overnight, like lightning."

Figure 1.1 suggests that one reason for the deep fall might be found in the preceding steep ascent. "What comes up must come down," seems appropriate here. Or as an expert expressed it, "The alpine wisdom on business cycles applies. Where the mountains are high, the valleys are deep."[9] From our current perspective it seems indeed illusive to expect that the rapid growth could have been sustained over an extended period of time. This applies as well to Chinese growth rates as to U.S. home prices, the global automotive industry or the excesses in Dubai. A striking example of steep ascent and fall is Cessna, the world market leader in private jets based in Wichita, Kansas. During the first half of 2008, order backlog continued to grow to $16 billion from $12.6 billion, an increase of 27%. Yet, what followed was an equally steep fall, when within a few weeks, lack of new orders and cancellations reduced the order backlog by 30% to 375 planes from 535.[10]

With the exception of the financial sector, 2008 still turned out to be a good year for most companies and industries. The strong growth of the first three quarters was not completely erased by the negative development towards the end of the year. The full impact of the crisis on volume, sales, and profits has only been experienced in 2009. In the context of the steep and strong decline, an important question is how long will the crisis likely last. Will the recession be over in a few months or will demand remain low for years to come? We will deal with this question in Chapter 9.

The purpose of this book is not to give a macroeconomic analysis of the causes of the current recession. Instead, we look at the crisis from the perspective of individual businesses. The aim is to help companies understand their situation better and to suggest quick and effective solutions to beat the crisis.

On the individual company level the main causes and effects of the crisis are as follows:

- Consumers are deeply unsettled and are saving their money instead of spending it. Purchases of products and services that are not immediately needed are postponed. We refer to such products and services as "postponables."
- The same applies to things that are "nice to have" but not really necessary. Purchases of "nice to have" items are either canceled

completely or cheaper means to satisfy these needs are chosen. Examples are luxury goods, extra equipment for cars, visits to restaurants, or vacation trips.

- The drop in in the demand for end products immediately affects the entire value chain. If no cars are bought, there are no orders for suppliers, who in turn order fewer intermediate products, machines, and raw materials.
- With some delay, jobs are lost, which causes the purchasing power of consumers to erode further, and the downward spiral intensifies.
- The loss in purchasing power is massively aggravated by the reduced willingness of financial institutions to grant loans. This credit crunch hits consumers and companies alike. For companies reduced credit equals reduced sales potential. Without credit insurance, many deliveries have to be canceled, they are simply too risky for the vendor.[11] This applies especially to exports.

How Badly Affected Are Specific Industries?

The crisis affects industries and companies in very different degrees. Therefore, managers must analyze the crisis not from a general perspective but from the point of view of their specific industry and company. Products and services that consumers need on an everyday basis are much less affected than "postponables" or "nice-to-have" items. In this context, a study that looked at the changes in American consumer spending in the recessions of 1990–1991 and 2001–2002 is highly revealing. Figure 1.2 shows the results.

The overall growth of demand during the two former crises was 10% lower than the growth of demand for the comparison period 1984–2006. Given the variation across sectors, however, it would be misleading to look at averages here. In this study the hardest-hit sector was "food outside of home," a "nice-to-have" product. At the same time, "food at home" grew considerably. During former recessions, the demand for groceries actually increased. The increase of spending for education is surprising. When the job market is bad, young people tend to prolong their professional training or studies, get additional qualifications or apply for MBA programs.

Even within an industry, subsectors can be differently affected. The machinery industry is generally considered to be strongly affected by the current crisis. But even this generalization is incorrect, as Figure 1.3 illustrates. A look at the subsectors reveals extreme differences.

Fig. 1.2: The growth of selected industries in former crises

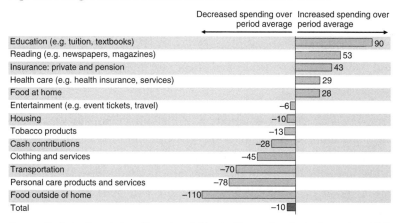

	Decreased spending over period average ←	→ Increased spending over period average
Education (e.g. tuition, textbooks)		90
Reading (e.g. newspapers, magazines)		53
Insurance: private and pension		43
Health care (e.g. health insurance, services)		29
Food at home		28
Entertainment (e.g. event tickets, travel)	−6	
Housing	−10	
Tobacco products	−13	
Cash contributions	−28	
Clothing and services	−45	
Transportation	−70	
Personal care products and services	−78	
Food outside of home	−110	
Total	−10	

Source: "Industry Trends in a Downturn," *The McKinsey Quarterly*, December 2008.
A comparison of the average growth of consumer spending in the recessions 1990–1991 and
2001–2002 to the average change from 1984 to 2006. Index for the average growth in the entire
period = 0

Fig. 1.3: Deviations from average growth rate in subsectors of the machinery industry

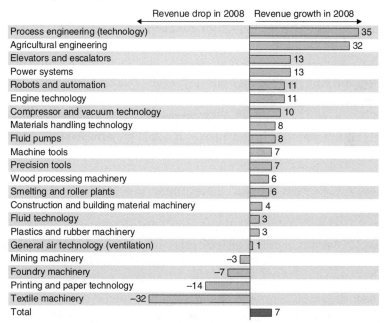

	Revenue drop in 2008 ←	→ Revenue growth in 2008
Process engineering (technology)		35
Agricultural engineering		32
Elevators and escalators		13
Power systems		13
Robots and automation		11
Engine technology		11
Compressor and vacuum technology		10
Materials handling technology		8
Fluid pumps		8
Machine tools		7
Precision tools		7
Wood processing machinery		6
Smelting and roller plants		6
Construction and building material machinery		4
Fluid technology		3
Plastics and rubber machinery		3
General air technology (ventilation)		1
Mining machinery	−3	
Foundry machinery	−7	
Printing and paper technology	−14	
Textile machinery	−32	
Total		7

Source: Verband Deutscher Maschinen- und Anlagenbau e.V. (VDMA), Frankfurt 2009

The difference between a 35% revenue growth in process engineering and a 32% decline for textile machinery makes it clear that looking at averages is completely pointless. We observe similar deviations between subsectors in automotive, banks, or retail. In-depth analysis and understanding of causes and effects are indispensable.

The consequences for individual companies vary even more strongly. At the end of the day, it counts for a manager how his or her company is affected. It is entirely possible that a company grows in a shrinking industry or declines in a growing industry. Changes in the market position are particularly frequent in times of crisis. Market shares are redistributed in bad times, not in good times. When business is good everybody gets along easily and market shares don't change much. If the market shrinks, however, the weaker competitors often exit the market. This is the opportunity for the stronger ones to improve their market position. This pattern is similar to the hypothesis of the late evolution biologist Stephen Jay Gould, who claimed that evolution does not happen in a uniformly continuous way, but in leaps (theory of punctuated equilibrium).[12] Long phases with little development are followed by short periods of abrupt change. This hypothesis can also be applied to markets.[13]

An elite group of companies, the so-called hidden champions, definitely confirms this theory.[14] A majority of the managers of these companies say that the development of their companies occurred in leaps. Many have survived serious crises during their existence, 30% of them grave ones. This is why the hidden champions do not panic in view of the current crisis but react with relative calm. One reason is that with an equity ratio of 42% they are very solidly financed.[15] Many hidden champions expect to emerge from the crisis stronger than before. However, to achieve that goal they have to navigate around dangerous obstacles, act prudently and, above all, avoid grave mistakes.

How Are Certain Product Categories Affected?

We have seen that the crisis hits above all "postponables" and "nice to haves." But this is only a general rule of thumb. Every company has to take an in-depth look at the causes in order to understand its individual situation. This helps to anticipate further developments and is, above all, an essential requirement for the definition of quick solutions for the problems at hand. How are selected industries challenged by and coping with the crisis?

Durable Consumer Goods

Most durable consumer goods fall into the category of "postponables" and suffer badly from the crisis. Cars, household appliances, consumer electronics, computers, or furniture are typical examples. But even here a differentiated look seems indicated. For example, an increased ecological awareness, a growing social stigmatization of driving cars (particularly big ones), high gasoline prices, and an overall tighter budget can cause many people to use public transportation or the bicycle to go to work. This would lead to an increased demand for bicycles and bicycle-related services. A study among bicycle dealers revealed that this is indeed the case. The same is true for do-it-yourself and home improvement products. Higher unemployment and tighter budgets foster demand in home improvement stores. If fewer washing machines are sold, the existing ones need to be repaired more often. Low-cost repair shops experience higher demand during bad times.

Automotive

The automotive industry is one of the sectors that has been most severely hit by the crisis. The press coverage has been extensive and doesn't have to be reiterated here. For some companies sales are down more than one third. After the onset of the crisis many car manufacturers reacted prudently and quickly by reducing capacities and cutting costs. But sales losses of 40% or more cannot be offset on the cost side. To ensure survival, sales and marketing activities should have been ramped up immediately – and not been confined to margin-ruining discounts. To this day, the author has not seen that such measures have been enacted. By chance, his own leasing contract ran out in the spring of 2009 so that he was "in the market." Has he received any calls from car dealers of other brands? Has he received mail from car manufacturers? Was he offered test drives? Did any of the numerous automotive managers he knows try to sell him a car? Did he receive telephone calls from underemployed internal staffers? Did a representative of the brand his wife bought a few months earlier contact him to find out whether he was interested to switch to that brand? Was there an offer of a leasing contract with three months free (as had been the case for an office building)? Did car sellers try to make an appointment to visit him at home? Did a car company offer the author's employees a small fleet of cars for test drives over the weekend? The author has to answer all these questions with a "no." And yet, all these quick solutions would have been legal and possible. And at the same time, thousands and thousands of highly qualified employees of the car companies were sitting idly in their offices – or were laid off.

Fast-Moving Consumer Goods

Products of everyday use, such as food, beverages or washing powder, are less affected by the crisis. The same applies to pharmaceuticals, utilities, or telecommunications. The more the products satisfy basic daily needs the harder it is for consumers to do without them. A sick person is not going to refrain from seeing a doctor because of the crisis. A trip to the hairdresser is unavoidable from time to time. A vacation trip to a distant paradise, on the other hand, can be easily postponed or replaced by a less-expensive holiday closer to home. Confectionery, chocolate, and salty snacks may even be bought in higher quantities because of increased leisure time or stress. Services require a more detailed inspection. The CEO of a European cinema chain says that his company profits from the crisis. Interestingly he did not argue that people have more time to go to the movies, but that "it is cheaper for a young man to take his girl-friend to see a film than to a restaurant."

Financial Services

The crisis creates an increased demand for personal security. Figure 1.2 showed that health insurance, other types of insurance, as well as old age provisions grew strongly in earlier crises. However, the need for security is counterbalanced by restricted financial means. Complex financial offers such as certificates and trust funds caved in massively after the subprime disaster. Apart from a greater aversion to risks, the complexity and intransparency of many financial products impede consumer acceptance. Whether complex products will be permanently damaged by the crisis remains to be seen. A quick recovery should not be expected. On the other hand, simple and secure types of investments such as federal bonds are profiting. Banks and insurances need to make special efforts to revitalize their businesses.

Industrial Goods

Similar to consumer goods, there are industrial goods that are required at a specific moment, and others that are "postponable." Spare parts or repair services are required when a machine is broken. The replacement of an old but still intact machine, on the other hand, can be postponed. Accordingly, demand for machines and plant equipment has collapsed. Caterpillar, an industrial icon, reports a fall in revenue of 22% for the first quarter in 2009.[16] Intel's revenue fell 26% in the same period of time. A critical issue in this context is "derived demand." A car needs exactly two outside rear view mirrors. The order for these mirrors is caused by the purchase of the car – and by nothing else. This demand is not original, but derived. This simple fact deserves highest attention since it is decisive for the degree to which sales can be influenced. Exactly two mirrors are needed per car, not more, not less. In contrast to tires or brake pads, there is no significant aftermarket. The demand for outside rear view mirrors is tied directly to the number of cars that are sold. When fewer cars are ordered the manufacturer of the mirrors has no way to sell more mirrors. He can try to win over new customers or to increase his market share with current customers, but such measures usually don't work in the short term. The same applies to many other products (e.g., one heating system per house, one hard-drive per computer), but also to services, such as the transportation of a new car from the factory to the dealer. Products with derived demand are as hard hit by the crisis as the end-products. A drop in demand for the end-product or for the "postponable" is reflected throughout the entire value chain. And there is little the manufacturer of a "derived demand" product can do to alleviate the sales slump.

Healthcare

Healthcare is a huge sector accounting for 12–15% of the gross domestic product in advanced countries. Although sick people need medical treatment, the health care sector has experienced the crisis too. Rising unemployment and stagnating or falling salaries curtail the resources of health insurers and the budgets for hospitalization or doctor appointments. Hospitals and physicians postpone new investments. Insurance companies use new methods of cost reduction (discount contracts, invitations to tender). Patients exert pressure on manufacturers as well. For products that are not covered by the health insurance we observe higher price sensitivity and partially decreasing demand. These can include dental implants, prostheses, eyeglasses, and cosmetic treatments. Even in the healthcare sector increased efforts in marketing and sales are necessary to face the crisis. Due to the different health systems, the impact of the current crisis strongly differs from country to country.

Telecommunications and IT

In advanced countries the market for telecommunications and IT typically contributes between 5 and 10% to gross domestic products.[17] A little less than half of this is for telecommunication services and products, the other half for IT services, equipment and software. Consumer electronics account for less than 10% of this market. The impact of the crisis on the subsectors is very different. Telecommunications services are less affected. In the beginning, the crisis did not cause any noticeable reduction of telephone or Internet services.[18] Data traffic even continued to increase up to 20% annually. In the further course of the crisis, however, telephone and data traffic show increasing signs of weakness. In B2B business, price pressure is increasing, however, as the budgets of industrial customers become tighter. Much harder hit are hardware manufacturers (e.g., cell phones, personal computers) with sales losses of up to 20%, as well as suppliers of business software. These products are "postponables." The current recession differs from the burst of the "Internet bubble" in 2001/2002 when the telecommunications and IT sectors were at the center of the crisis and exposed to its full impact. In the current crisis they are in a more peripheral position and are affected less than average.

Chemicals

As a supplier to the automotive and electronic industry, the chemical industry is hard hit by the crisis. On the other hand, the pharmaceutical sector has a stabilizing effect. On the whole, the industry expects a relatively moderate production decrease of less than 5%, but, because of simultaneously sinking prices, a stronger revenue loss of well over 5%.[19] Many companies quickly adjusted their capacities to the reduced demand. BASF, Dupont, Dow, Bayer, Merck, Lanxess, Clariant, and others shut down capacities. Lyondell was the first large corporation to file for bankruptcy. New capacities, especially in China, cause further price pressures for basic chemicals. Some products are sold at marginal costs. Prices for special chemicals are somewhat more stable, but are also declining because of the tight budgets in the automotive and electronic industries.

Tourism

Tourism used to be seen as the largest industry in the world. Holiday trips were considered the growth markets of recent decades. The crisis has a strong negative effect on holiday trips, which are classical "nice-to-haves." A decreasing number of bookings, a preference for shorter trips, and last minute bookings are worrying tour operators. While these tendencies are not completely new, they have become much more pronounced in the crisis. "We have never had such a bad booking curve before, not even after 9/11," is a typical comment. Given the increased preference for last-minute bookings, tour operators who know how to handle the interaction between free capacities and price are at a clear advantage. So far, tour operators have managed to compensate for the lower number of passengers by cutting capacities and stabilizing prices.[20] By reducing capacities in the crisis tour operators have acted intelligently. The industry needs to avoid a further drop in prices with negative margin effects.

Media

The media are suffering badly from the crisis because negative structural and cyclical trends coexist. Structurally, the traditional media such as print and television are losing ground to the Internet, especially to Google. The readership of traditional print media is declining. In 1964, 81% of adult Americans read a daily newspaper; today less than 50% retain this habit.[21] Besides readers or viewers the second revenue source, advertising, is drying up. Advertising is a "postponable." Magazines and newspapers report strong declines in advertising revenue. For the first quarter of 2009, in the U.S., advertising revenues were 28.2% lower and in the U.K. 38.7% lower than in the previous year. Help-wanted ads even dropped 62%.[22] The number of paid advertising pages in *USA Today* sank to 527 from 826, a decline of 36%, in that quarter. Many of the print advertisements that appear are not even fully paid. Volume and price reductions add to each other. Several newspapers and many magazines have already thrown in the towel. Many more will follow them. Media companies who want to survive have to fight on the revenue front. Cost cuts alone will not save them.

Luxury Products

The situation for luxury products is heterogeneous. On the one hand, luxury products continue to be bought by affluent customers whose purchasing power has been less harmed by the crisis than that of lower income groups. On the other hand, even some of the better-off customers can only afford luxury products during good times. The crisis has diminished the net worth of many of these individuals. Comments on the luxury goods industry are accordingly diverse. "Luxury industry goes astray" was one headline when Richemont, the world's second-largest luxury goods company, announced a marked drop in revenues with no improvement in sight. The world's largest luxury manufacturer LVMH, on the other hand, continues to send optimistic messages.

Subsectors of the luxury goods industry are affected to varying degrees. Leather products such as shoes or handbags are more resistant to the crisis than jewelry or watches. A. Lange & Soehne, makers of very expensive luxury watches, reduced work hours but sees good long-term prospects.[23] Traditional brands are less affected by the crisis than brands that have lost their exclusiveness by purveying to the volume market. "There is a trend towards established brands and high-quality products," says luxury fund manager Andrea Gers. Despite the crisis, Ferrari expects 2009 to be a record year. Production capacities are sold out until 2011.

Luxury goods are not restricted to the private sector. An example that illustrates the impact of the crisis on "commercial luxury goods" are private jets. In recent years these airplanes were bought above all by companies and experienced an enormous boom. Private jets are exemplary for luxury and convenience, but also for business efficiency. In the current crisis, this industry has crashed. Until recently the global market leader Cessna had orders for 535 planes. However, within a few weeks many of these orders were canceled, and simultaneously new orders plummeted. Cessna now expects 375 deliveries, a reduction of 30%. An improvement is not in sight and at the same time the number of used airplanes offered on the market skyrocketed to 2,788 (+65%); 16% of all private jets currently in use are up for sale. As a result, prices went into free fall. A used Cessna "Citation X" is 28% cheaper today than it was three years ago.[24] This price erosion impedes the sale of new airplanes at reasonable prices. Customers demand markedly bigger discounts.

Discount Products

On the other side of the price range are low-cost or discount products. A common notion is that discount stores are "the great winners in the crisis."[25] However, again a differentiated perspective is indicated. Generally, the low-cost segment is indeed profiting from the crisis for two reasons. First, due to their decreasing purchasing power, customers of these products are forced to buy even more low-cost products than before. Second, customers who did not buy in this segment before are now turning to the discount segment. Despite these promising prospects, we observe intensive competition in this segment. In Chapter 9, we look at the possible emergence of a new ultra-low-price segment. It is possible that leading discounters are already fighting for supremacy in this emerging segment.

The fact that the low-price segment as a whole is likely to profit from the crisis does not mean that the chances of survival for individual companies have improved. The opposite is probably the case. In this segment (e.g., low-cost airlines, tour operators, dealers) there are numerous marginal players who cannot compete in an increased price competition with companies who have streamlined their operations to extreme efficiency. A well-known casualty is the retailer Woolworth, which in the spring of 2009 filed for bankruptcy both in the U.K. and Germany. Despite the volume increase this segment is undergoing a very tough selection process.

Effects of Government Programs

In the course of the crisis enormous government subsidies have been mobilized. The long-term results with regard to public debt and inflation will be discussed in Chapter 9. Figure 1.4 provides an overview of selected programs that amount to gigantic sums worldwide.

According to Bloomberg, public capital injections, liquidity assistance, and credit guarantees add up to $10,000 billion in the U.S. alone.[26] The largest program relative to the gross domestic product was

Fig. 1.4: Selected government programs

Germany	USA	France	Japan	China
$105.3 billion (81 billion €)	$789.5 billion (ca. 612 billion €)	$33.8 billion (26 billion €)	81.6 billion ¥ (ca. $806 billion, ca. 620 billion €)	4 billion ¥ (ca. $611 billion, ca. 470 billion €) 2nd package planned
• Investment into infrastructure and buildings • Tax reductions • Reduction of health insurance premiums • Short-time subsidies • Scrapping bonus • Umbrella for companies	• Investment into infrastructure and buildings • Tax reductions • Creation of jobs • Health insurance subsidies	• Investment into infrastructure and buildings • One-time payment to low-income households • Scrapping bonus for cars	• Tax reductions • One-time payments • Employment schemes • Investment into infrastructure and buildings • Support for banks	• Investment into infrastructure and buildings • Investment into social development programs • Investment into environmental protection and disaster control • Tax reductions

probably launched by China.[27] The more than $600 billion amount to approximately 15% of the Chinese gross domestic product.[28]

Most countries adopted industry-specific programs. Germany was a pioneer with its "scrapping bonus" of $3,250 per traded-in old car, introduced in the spring of 2009.[29] Germany allotted about $6.5 billion to this program, and two million cars have been bought under this stimulus package. The U.S. followed in June 2009 with a similar package, called "Cash for Clunkers" (the official name is Consumer Assitance to Recycle and Save or, in short, CARS). Consumers who trade in gas guzzlers for more fuel-efficient cars receive $3,500 to $4,500. The "Cash for Clunkers" program immediately drove car sales up.[30] A large part of the public money goes into construction and infrastructure projects (roads, railroads, schools, etc.), which take time to implement. However, it can be expected that the gigantic programs will show first results soon.

Many of the government programs are questionable with regard to their results. Subsidies for cars, as applied in the U.S., Germany, Italy, France, Japan, China, and other countries, favor only the automotive sector. Other industries that also sell "postponables" and are equally hard-hit by the crisis, such as household appliances, would have been just as eligible for public financial support. In fact, one union has demanded a "scrapping bonus for refrigerators" and Bosch-CEO Fehrenbach suggested a scrapping bonus for old heating systems.[31] Protests against the car subsidies came from the retail industry. "The government redirects consumer money to the automotive industry," complained one of the representatives.[32] Discussions also focused on whether customers should be given money directly (e.g., consumption vouchers in Japan, subsidies in the U.S.), whether companies should be subsidized (as is the case in the French and U.S. automotive industries), or whether credit guarantees for companies should be issued (German program of $100 billion). Equally controversial is the question whether direct payments to customers or tax reductions (e.g., the value added tax reduction to 15% from 17.5% in the U.K., which amounts to a 2.5% price cut across all product categories, or a reduction of the sales tax for small cars to 5% from 10% in China) are more effective.[33]

Experience shows that all state interventions should be viewed skeptically. The intentions may be good. The problem is the implementation. Niall Ferguson, economic historian at Harvard University, commented on the U.S. program: "The American Congress has managed to turn the great program of public spending into a horse-trade. To ask Congress to spend $800 billion in a sensible manner is like asking a group of alcoholics to run a bar. I believe that this package will have little or no macroeconomic effect."[34]

From a company's perspective these discussions are not very helpful. The programs are what they are. All companies have to analyze the effect of the public spending on their own markets and how they can get the best deal out of it. Apart from the automotive industry, the construction industry and its highly diversified suppliers will probably profit most. This is a considerable part of a modern national economy, for building materials and modern construction technologies include numerous sub-industries. Closely connected is energy savings because a considerable part of the investments will go into this sector, for example, into wind and solar power. Last but not least, important parts of the machinery industry (commercial vehicles, construction machines) will profit indirectly when demand in the construction and energy industries turns around.

Putting the Crisis into Perspective

The current crisis is without any doubt the most severe recession since the Great Depression. One expert contends that "the crisis erases the global domestic product of an entire year."[35] The Asian Development Bank (ADP) estimates the loss in asset values at $50,000 billion dollars (the U.S. gross domestic product in 2008 was $14,265 billion).[36] The World Bank expects global economic performance to go down for the first time since World War II. And there is no lack of gloomy predictions. Niall Ferguson, economic historian at Harvard University, says, "We are experiencing the financial symptoms of a world war."[37] Fortune columnist Geoff Colvin foresees "a recession of biblical proportions."[38] Christian Bubb, CEO of construction giant Implenia, speaks of "apocalyptical dimensions" of the crisis.[39] In a recent workshop, the CEO of one of the world's largest automotive companies consistently spoke of "global depression." A bankruptcy expert openly discusses a "monetary reform as a radical consequence" of the crisis.[40] A high-ranking official openly talked of a 10% property levy to reduce public debt. Expropriation is no longer a taboo. Even America is practicing "nationalization."[41] Others deal with the problem differently, such as John Nonbye, CEO of the traffic sign manufacturer Nonbye. He simply prohibited the use of the word "crisis" in his company.[42]

In spite of these fears, the crisis should be put into perspective. A few sober remarks seem indicated. Gross domestic products in advanced

Fig. 1.5: Exports of Germany, China and the U.S. – putting the crisis into perspective

in billion US-$

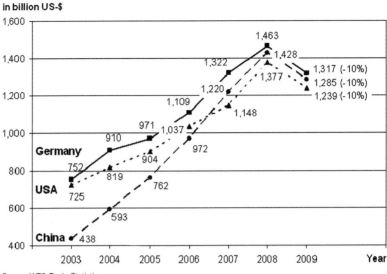

Source: WTO Trade Statistics

countries are expected to decline between 2 and 7% in 2009.[43] This would be the strongest decline since World War II. However, China and India still expect positive growth between 5 and 8%.[44] In the first half of 2009 China's economy actually grew 6%.

Strong declines are also predicted for exports. The World Bank forecasts a decline of 3% in the global trade volume.[45] To put the crisis into perspective, we look at the development of the exports of the three largest exporters since 2003; that is, the last six years. Figure 1.5 shows the numbers. In all these years Germany has been consistently the largest exporter. German exports are expected to go down between 8 and 15% in 2009, which seems a dramatic decline.[46] Still, Germany is expected to remain number one for several years.

If we assume a decline of 10% in 2009 for these three leading export nations, all exports would still be well above the 2006 exports and about 70% above the 2003 level. For China, exports would even be 190% above the 2003 figure. Relative to the longer-term development, the decline in 2009 looks rather moderate. One of our problems is that all comparisons are made on an annual basis. A record in the preceding year automatically raises the bar. And the bar in 2008 is historically extremely high. In this sense a prudent voice from the engineering sector states "the negative values have to be partially attributed to the extremely positive development in the preceding year."[47] This applies to exports, car sales, machinery, and many other markets that all set outstanding historical record levels in 2008. A similar argument is true for certain price developments, for example, agricultural products. Although prices have dropped from year-ago levels "the glass is half full, not half empty, as the prices are still higher than they were two or three years ago," says Theo Jachmann of pesticide producer Syngenta.[48] Even oil prices are still high compared to historical levels. Another driver of the collapse in new orders is the reduction of inventory by customers. Customers whose sales are stagnating make fewer purchases and allow their warehouses to empty.[49]

These considerations should not be understood as an attempt to play down the crisis but to gain a more sober perspective. The problem is not only the crisis itself but how it is perceived and dealt with. One of the most serious aspects is its impact on the job market. Unemployment is going to increase sharply.[50] Also, averages mean very little, as the examples in Figures 1.2 and 1.3 have clearly shown. A decrease in the gross domestic product of 5% can mean that some industries grow by 20% while others decline by 30%. For those who strongly decline the situation is, of course, really critical.

How Has Customer Behavior Changed?

Around the year 2000 the advent of the Internet resulted in an atmosphere of euphoria that is hard to understand for someone who did not witness it. The magic word was "new economy" and even prudent observers expressed their conviction that the Internet had annihilated traditional economic laws and heralded a new economic age. Similar waves of collective euphoria or depression have occurred regularly throughout history, frequently causing widespread doubt about the validity of fundamental economic laws and causalities. "The world will never be the same again," is an often-heard comment in the current crisis.[51] Such statements should be viewed with caution. The Internet has not invalidated traditional economic laws, and neither will the current crisis. While there is plenty of reason to worry, a good deal of prudence seems indicated.

These remarks do not mean that customer behavior is not changing. The opposite is the case. It remains to be seen which of the behavioral and attitudinal changes will be temporary and which will be permanent. In our projects and studies we are observing the changes described below. They apply both to consumer goods and industrial goods, always with a grain of salt.

Fear of the Future

In this crisis, the customers' fear of the future strongly impacts their behavior and is difficult to overcome. Of the four marketing tools, product, price, communication, and distribution, none emerges as a simple, effective means of overcoming customers' reluctance or refusal to buy. Price is the most likely candidate, but when resistance to buying is very strong, prices have to be lowered so far that tiny or even negative margins result. This situation would be even worse for profitability than the slump in sales we are already witnessing.

Unfavorable Change in Price Elasticity

At first glance one might expect that price elasticity increases in a time of crisis. However, this applies only to price increases, not to price cuts. Price elasticity generally develops unfavorably during a crisis. Compared to more stable times, sales respond less positively to price cuts and more negatively to price increases. What's more, thresholds in the price demand curve are certain to shift. Prices have to be lowered by a considerably larger amount in order to enter the price-elastic part of the curve.

Hard Value and Cost Benefits Gain Importance

Hard value and cost benefits take on greater importance during a crisis. When times are good, customers are more likely to indulge in items that are "nice to have," but not really necessary. When times are tough, non-essential items start to feel the pinch. In this situation companies that can offer hard value or cost benefits may be able to boost their sales, revenue, and market share. A renowned engineering company, for example, reports that some customers are conducting projects despite the crisis, as long as these projects result in significant and fast cost savings. All investments related to more "cosmetic" modernization, on the other hand, have been stopped. Elsewhere, a crop protection company is driving a product that is slightly less effective and less environmentally friendly than other more innovative products, but still fulfills its purpose. The advantage is that this product is applied just once each season, cutting farmers' labor costs significantly. In spite of the crisis, the company has increased not only its revenue, but also its market share.

Compressed Time Preference

Time preferences are changing, with short-term effects winning over long-term effects. We refer to this as a "compressed" time preference. A major bank offered an investment product that guaranteed a high after-tax return, but only after five years. The product failed because in uncertain times investors are wary of tying up their money for the long term. The bank therefore redesigned its offering and shortened the payback period. Even though the return is lower now, the product sells much better. The situation is similar for industrial goods. Willingness to invest falls dramatically in times of crisis, but rapid savings are loved by B2B customers. Sales departments need to give immediate savings a higher priority, and perhaps even rework the business model to focus more strongly on short-term benefits.

Financing Becomes More Important

Financing and payment conditions are becoming increasingly important. Many customers are facing a restricted cash flow, and postponing payments helps to relieve their liquidity problems. This opens up a competitive advantage for vendors that can afford to be generous on this front. A manufacturer of household goods, for example, started offering more liberal financing and more flexible payment targets, and was able to raise prices as a result. The company considerably boosted its margins, even after hedging its greater financial exposure by factoring.

Safety Moves to the Forefront

Safety is becoming an increasingly important requirement, especially in the financial sector. The crisis has made bonds with top ratings more popular despite their low returns. Companies that are in unstable conditions have great difficulties in selling their products. Nobody wants to buy a car, a household appliance, or a machine and learn shortly after the purchase that the supplier is filing for bankruptcy.

In general, preferences for safety and security are expected to become even more pronounced in the future. This definitely applies to financially "safe" products with guaranteed returns. But it is also true for travel destinations. As more people decide to take vacations in close locations, these regions will benefit at the expense of more remote destinations, particularly when those are considered to be less safe. Similarly, demand for security products and services increases when a rise in crime and social tensions is expected. Manufacturers of safes, fences, and alarm systems report strong growth rates during crises. Safety in its many forms will be become a major contributor to value.

The crisis therefore has wide-ranging effects on customer behavior. The new situation is making it considerably harder for companies to do business. But changing customer needs also pave the way for promising courses of immediate action.

Summary

The crisis reveals complex causes and effects. Understanding them is of crucial importance for companies to make rational decisions. We summarize the main insights from this chapter as follows:

- The current crisis is a sales crisis and must be fought at the sales front. Of course, costs have to be lowered as well.
- Customers are deeply unsettled and refuse to buy. This reluctance to buy extends to the entire economy.
- Individual industries and companies are affected to extremely varying degrees. "Postponables" and "nice to haves" are suffering most.
- Some products and services profit from the crisis and keep on growing. But even within the same industry we observe enormous differences in this regard.
- Customer behavior is undergoing multiple changes. Besides a general fear of the future, unfavorable changes in price elasticity, a compressed time preference, higher importance of hard values, financing, and safety can be observed.

The crisis has varied consequences on the behavior of customers and competitors. On the whole, the changes make it harder to do business.

However, those who have an early understanding of changing customer requirements and are responsive can actually profit from the crisis.

Endnotes

1 Geoff Colvin, "A Recession of Biblical Dimensions," *Fortune*, February 16, 2009.

2 "Billig lohnt sich," sueddeutsche.de, February 3, 2009.

3 Philip Grothe and Grigori Bokeria, "Internationale Wachstumsstudie: Strategien und Herausforderungen für Industrieunternehmen – Schock oder Wachstum trotz Krise?" Study by Simon-Kucher & Partners, Bonn, January 2009.

4 Marcus Jauer, "Welt von gestern," *Frankfurter Allgemeine Zeitung*, February 14, 2009, p. 40.

5 Philip Kotler und John A. Caslione *Chaotics: The Business of Managing and Marketing in the Age of Turbulence*, New York: AMACOM 2009.

6 Most experts date the beginning of the crisis to August 7, 2007. On that day, interbank interest rates took a giant upward leap of 70 basis points. The normal oscillation is within single-digit basis points limits.

7 For a detailed description, see Nathan Lewis, *Gold: The Once and Future Money*, Hoboken, New Jersey: Wiley 2007.

8 B2B stands for "Business to Business," i.e., business between companies; B2C means "Business to Consumers."

9 Stefan Kooths, German Institute for Economic Research, April 18, 2009.

10 "Fliegende Symbole der Verschwendung," *Frankfurter Allgemeine Zeitung*, February 10, 2009, p. 12.

11 A credit insurance covers the risk if a customer does not pay despite of delivery of the goods.

12 Stephen Jay Gould, *The Structure of Evolutionary Theory*, New York: Belknap Press 2002.

13 Interview with the author in *Impulse*, February 27, 2008.

14 Hermann Simon, *Hidden Champions of the 21st Century*, New York: Springer 2009. Hidden Champions are little-known world market leaders with revenue below $4 billion.

15 The equity ratio is the ratio of equity to total assets.

16 "Caterpillar Posts Loss, Cuts Outlook," WSJ.com, April 22, 2009.

17 BITKOM, ITK market data, December 2008.

18 Ekkehard Stadie, Hanna Jesse, "'Lipstick Effect' auch in der Mobilfunk industrie," Simon-Kucher & Partners, Bonn, January 2009.

19 "Wenig Hoffnung für die Chemie," *Frankfurter Allgemeine Zeitung*, March 11, 2009, p. 13.

20 See, for example, "Air Berlin: Mehr Passagiere und höhere Auslastung in 2008," press release by Air Berlin, January 7, 2009.

21 Nicholas Carr, *The Big Switch: Rewiring the World*, New York: Norton 2008.

22 *Financial Times*, April 17, 2009, p. 8.

23 "Kurzarbeit bei Lange & Soehne," *Frankfurter Allgemeine Zeitung*, March 5, 2009. p. 16.

24 "Fliegende Symbole der Verschwendung," *Frankfurter Allgemeine Zeitung*, February 10, 2009, p. 12.

25 "Billig lohnt sich," sueddeutsche.de, February 3, 2009.

26 "Ein ketzerischer Vorschlag," *Financial Times Deutschland*, February 12, 2009, p. 15.

27 "China stemmt sich gegen die Krise," Zeit Online, February 2, 2009.

28 The gross domestic product of China in 2008 was 30.067 trillion Yuan (about $3,900 billion); cf. "China's GDP grows 9% in 2008," Xinhua News Agency, January 22, 2009.

29 In early 2009, the German government started a program where anyone who owns a car that is nine years or older scraps it and buys a new car receives 2,500 Euros, which corresponds to $3,250.

30 "Cash for Clunkers," *Time*, August 17, 2009, p. 18.

31 "Die Kurzarbeit ist ein teures Werkzeug", Interview with Franz Fehrenbach, CEO of Robert Bosch, *Frankfurter Allgemeine Zeitung*, March 14, 2009, p. 16.

32 "Abwrackprämie erzürnt den Handel," *Handelsblatt*, March 6, 2009.

33 In November 2008, the author and a high-ranking government official recommended that VAT be canceled Germany for one entire month. This measure would probably have had massive effects. However, it would have had to be implemented in the entire European Union, where a minimum VAT of 15% is dictated by law. This is why the U.K. lowered its VAT to "only" 15%.

34 "Wir erleben die finanziellen Symptome eines Weltkriegs," Interview with Niall Ferguson, *Frankfurter Allgemeine Zeitung*, February 24, 2009.

35 "Die Krise vernichtet die Wirtschaftsleistung eines Jahres," *Frankfurter Allgemeine Zeitung*, March 10, 2009, p. 11.

36 ibid.

37 "Wir erleben die finanziellen Symptome eines Weltkriegs," Interview with Niall Ferguson, *Frankfurter Allgemeine Zeitung*, February 24, 2009.

38 Geoff Colvin, "A Recession of Biblical Proportions," *Fortune*, February 16, 2009, p. 15.

39 "Kampf der Krise," *Bilanz*, February 2009, p. 29.

40 "Währungsreform als radikalste Folge," *General-Anzeiger Bonn*, March 7, 2009, p. 9.

41 Otto Graf Lambsdorff, "Enteignung: Nicht Ultima Ratio, sondern Offenbarungseid," *Frankfurter Allgemeine Zeitung*, March 4, 2009, p. 12.

42 "Schluss mit depressiv – Betrieb verbietet 'Finanzkrise'", n-tv.de, January 27, 2009.

43 The German government expects a decline of 2.3%, the German Institute for Economic Research –3%. Uwe Angenendt, Chief Economist of BHF-Bank, thinks a decrease of more than 4% is possible. Cf. "Harter Abschwung kostet viele Jobs; Experten rechnen für 2009 mit einer stärkeren Rezession und höherer Arbeitslosigkeit," *Berliner Zeitung*, February 17, 2009, p. 9, and "Japans Wirtschaft im freien Fall," *Financial Times Deutschland*, February 17, 2009, p. 1. Professor Norbert Walter expects –5%, cf. "Der Verfolgte," *Frankfurter Allgemeine Zeitung*, February 24, 2009, p. 16. Joerg Kraemer, Chief Economist of Commerzbank, even talks about –6 to –7%, cf. FAZ.NET, March 23, 2009. Similar declines are expected for other countries: France: at least –1%, USA: –2%, Russia: –2.2%, England: –3.6%, Japan: –3.8%.

44 "Frankreichs BIP schrumpft um 1,2 Prozent," Capital.de, February 13, 2009; "Russlands Wirtschaftsministerium senkt erneut BIP- und Industrieprognose", RIA Novosti, February 17, 2009; "China verkündet Wachstumsziel von 8 Prozent", Spiegel Online, March 5, 2009; "United Kingdom at a Glance: 2009–10," Country Forecast Select, Economist Intelligence Unit, February 11, 2009; "United States at a Glance: 2009–10," Country Forecast Select, Economist Intelligence Unit, February 4, 2009; "India at a Glance: 2009–10," Country Forecast Select, Economist Intelligence Unit, February 2, 2009; "Economic Data Japan," Economist Intelligence Unit, February 17, 2009.

45 "Die Krise vernichtet die Wirtschaftsleistung eines Jahres," *Frankfurter Allgemeine Zeitung*, March 10, 2009, p. 11.

46 "Deutschlands Ausfuhr ist um 20 Prozent gefallen," *Frankfurter Allgemeine Zeitung*, March 11, 2009, p. 11, and "Exporteure erwarten stärksten Einbruch seit 60 Jahren," Spiegel Online, March 24, 2009.

47 "Maschinenbau erhält drastisch weniger Aufträge," *Frankfurter Allgemeine Zeitung*, March 5, 2009, p. 11.

48 "Das Geschäft brummt," *Die Welt*, February 26, 2009.

49 "Infineon startet Geschäftsjahr tief in den roten Zahlen," Associated Press Worldstream – German, February 6, 2009.

50 "Gut gemeint, schlecht gemacht", Interview with Christoph Schmidt, *Wirtschaftswoche*, February 9, 2009, p. 25, and "Harter Abschwung kostet viele Jobs; Experten rechnen für 2009 mit einer stärkeren Rezession und höherer Arbeitslosigkeit," *Berliner Zeitung*, February 17, 2009, p. 9.

51 The German Minister of Finance, Peer Steinbrueck, in a policy statement on the situation of financial markets said to the German Parliament on September 25, 2008, "The world will never again be as it was before the crisis."

Chapter 2

What Works and What Doesn't Work Against the Crisis

In the current crisis, there is no shortage of advice and recommendations. And yet, the same standard solutions that are pitched in times of stability are also being put forth during the crisis: innovation, growth, market share gains, and so on. Unfortunately, this kind of advice is not only useless but can prove outright dangerous in the midst of a downturn of this magnitude. Solutions that require high initial investments and promise to generate positive cash flows years later will help companies little in the short term to survive the crisis. These solutions may actually put companies at even greater risk of failure. What companies need now are solutions that can be implemented quickly, have immediate effects, and improve profit and cash flow within weeks or months.

Understanding Supply and Demand

When we talk about a demand or sales crisis, we must first make sure that we understand the relationship between supply and demand — only then can we determine the most appropriate solutions. To better understand the current situation, let us first review the relationship between supply and demand during the most recent economic boom. During this phase demand in many industries was higher than supply (the available production capacity). This imbalance is depicted in Figure 2.1.

The situation, when demand consistently outstrips supply, is called a "seller's market." In a "seller's market," we typically observe the following consequences and behavior:

- Since production can't keep up with demand, delivery times increase. As a result, delivery becomes an increasingly important buying criterion for customers.
- Management focuses its attention on eliminating the bottlenecks in production and in the supply chain. Topics like customer orientation, service, or spare parts fade into the background.

H. Simon, *Beat the Crisis: 33 Quick Solutions for Your Company*,
DOI 10.1007/978-1-4419-0823-0_2, © Hermann Simon 2010

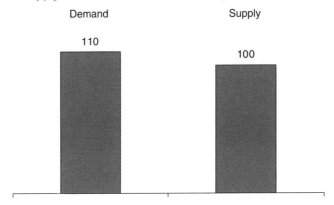
Fig. 2.1: Supply and demand in recent boom years

- Price increases are easy to implement and prices rise. The basic fact that demand outpaces supply indicates that market prices are too low, and suggests companies are failing to fully exploit the opportunity to raise prices.
- The sales force has an easy job – they just simply "allocate" the products.
- The sales force faces the risk of becoming arrogant with customers, who will in turn take their revenge when the economic expansion comes to an end and the next crisis sets in.

Of course, in an ideal world, supply and demand would always be in equilibrium. Yet in reality, this rarely occurs. More often, the economy has either too much or too little capacity. Equilibria are only reached during the short period between an economic expansion and an economic contraction.

In the current economic crisis, the fall in demand came suddenly and with great momentum. To help frame our discussion, we will assume that demand decreased to 75 from 110 (100=long-term average demand) once the economic downturn took effect. Relative to its value of 110 during the "boom years," demand has declined by 32%; relative to its long-term average, demand has declined by 25%. In the current crisis, these are realistic magnitudes for many industries and companies. At the same time demand was falling, supply, or production capacity, initially was unchanged at 100. According to the International Monetary Fund capacity utilization hovers around 69% in the U.S. (the lowest value since this indicator has been recorded in 1967) and 75% in Europe in 2009.[1] The situation illustrated in Figure 2.2 is thus very close to reality.

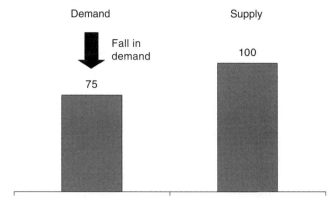

Fig. 2.2: Fall in demand in the crisis

What are the consequences of this dramatic change? What was once a sellers' market is now a pronounced "buyer's market." In other words, the power has shifted to buyers from sellers.

- Internally, companies are not fully utilizing capacity or employees, leading to reduced working hours, layoffs, and so on.
- Inventories rise: Manufactured products that have yet to be sold pile up in warehouses, factories, and stores.
- Downward price pressures mount – caused by customers exploiting their increased purchasing power and by competitors undercutting one another. Pressure to reduce prices also grows internally due to the need to get rid of surplus merchandise.
- Immediate cash flow is significantly more important than making new investments. Potential buyers hoard cash to survive the crisis by forgoing purchases and cutting costs.
- The sales force comes under greater pressure to increase sales. Since customers are more hesitant to make purchases, reaching sales targets becomes disproportionately more difficult.

The above discussion highlights how the current economic crisis, characterized by excess supply and diminishing demand, greatly affects all business aspects and profit drivers.

Profit Drivers and Their Effects

Solutions for beating the crisis must therefore involve all three profit drivers. We know from the previous chapter that there are only three such profit drivers: price, sales volume, and costs (costs can be subdivided into fixed and variable). How much influence or impact does each of the drivers have on profit? To illustrate this, we will use a simple example with a structure typical for manufactured products. Let's assume that the product price is $100 and the sales volume is 1 million units. The fixed costs are $30 million and the variable costs are $60 per unit. Given these figures, revenue equals $100 million and profit equals $10 million. Thus, the product is profitable and has a return on sales (or margin) of 10%. How does an isolated (ceteris paribus) 5% change in each profit driver affect profit? Figure 2.3 provides the answer.[2]

A 5% price increase generates a profit improvement of 50%. If the price is successfully increased to $105 without a loss in sales volume, then profit will increase by 50% to $15 million. Conversely, profit would decline by 50% to $5 million if the price were to decline by 5% given a constant sales volume. The percentage change in profit is ten times the change in price, giving price a profit lever of 10.[3] After price, variable unit costs are the second most effective profit driver. If the unit cost is reduced to $57 from $60, profit – ceteris paribus – increases by 30%. On the other hand, if variable unit costs were to increase by 5% (to $63 from $60), the profit would fall by an equivalent 30%. Therefore, the profit lever of variable costs is six. It is surprising that sales volume – with a profit lever of four – has a considerably lower profit impact than price. A 5% sales increase generates a profit improvement of only 20%, while a 5% price hike drives up profits by 50%. We see that in both cases, the revenue is identical: $105 million. For driving increased profit, a boost in revenue coming from a price hike is definitely much better than boosting revenue by increasing volume.

In a crisis, most companies experience falling prices and/or sales volumes rather than price or volume hikes. This means that the reverse implications come true. A 5% price decrease has a much stronger negative profit effect than a 5% sales drop; namely, 50% versus 20%. In terms of profit, it is definitely more advantageous to accept a sales decrease rather than a price decrease. The reason is easy to understand.

Fig. 2.3: Leverage of profit drivers

If the profit driver improves by 5%...	...profit changes by...
Price	50%
Variable unit costs	30%
Sales volume	20%
Fixed costs	15%

The negative effect of a price drop is fully reflected in the profit. The unit margin sinks to $5 from $10. Since in our calculation the sales volume and, thus, the variable costs are unchanged (the fixed costs are constant), profit decreases by the full 50%. The situation looks very different if sales volume falls 5% or 50,000 units. Here the variable costs decrease by $60×50,000=$3 million – meaning that profit plunges by "only" $2 million instead of by $5 million.

If a manager is confronted with these statements and given the choice between the following alternatives A or B, a dilemma becomes evident:

- Alternative A: Accept a 5% price drop (e.g., in the form of a discount) and maintain sales volume.
- Alternative B: Accept a 5% sales decrease and maintain the price level.

We have discussed these alternatives with hundreds of managers in seminars and workshops. Almost everyone prefers alternative A, even though it means that profits would drop by $3 million more than in alternative B. These managers defend their choice by arguing that they may not be able to win back their customers and their market share after the crisis subsides. Additionally, they claim that sales, market share, and subsequently employment would all prove higher with alternative A, thereby avoiding layoffs. First of all, a crisis at the current magnitude will offer growth potential to almost every company that survives the crisis without severe losses, once the respective industry starts to recover.[4] Second, we will show that there are better ways to avoid layoffs during a crisis than by maintaining sales volumes through drastic price cuts (see Chapters 3, 5, and 7). However, if there is already a preference in normal periods for the "lower price/higher sales volume" alternative, then this bias is likely to be much more pronounced during the crisis. In a downturn, companies are even more tempted to keep up sales, capacity utilization, and employment. Yet, these preferences and strategies are detrimental to profitability during a crisis. We refer the reader to specific literature that discusses the perennial conflict between profit on the one side and sales volume or market share on the other.[5]

Returning to our example, even if a company succeeds in lowering both the variable and fixed costs by 5%, the total profit effect would still be less than that of a 5% price improvement. Combined, both types of costs have a profit lever of nine; price alone has a lever of ten. In a crisis, price increases are difficult to achieve. But the same considerations apply to price defense and price stabilization. If the price is defended at a certain level – for example, accepting a price cut of only 5% instead of 10% – the same profit effects apply. Cost cutting and price defense deserve equal attention in the crisis. In practice, this equality is rarely observed. During a crisis, most managers instinctively focus on cost cutting. Further, many tend to actively cut prices, which is exactly the wrong thing to do.

There is another way to compare the profit drivers. To generate the same profit effect as a 5% price defense, the following improvements would have to be achieved:

- an 8.3% cut in variable costs
- a 12.5% increase in sales volume or
- a 16.7% cut in fixed costs

Admittedly, none of these improvements is easy to achieve in a crisis. But the comparison yields valuable insights. It highlights the importance of price as a profit driver and demonstrates why managers must fully utilize price to drive or defend profits during the crisis.

Our calculations demonstrate the interrelationship between profit and its drivers in the simplest way possible. The ceteris paribus assumption usually does not fully represent reality. The relationship between the profit drivers is typically more complicated and strongly dependent on the specific situation – which is why a thorough analysis of the individual case is necessary to arrive at the right, quick solutions. Still, for insights into the magnitude of the profit drivers' impacts, the ceteris paribus assumption is a good starting point.

Each of the three profit drivers – price, sales volume, and costs – has a significant effect on profit. Therefore, managers should focus on all three in a crisis. For a product with a typical relation of fixed and variable costs, price is the strongest profit lever, followed by variable costs. Sales volume is a considerably weaker profit lever. Ultimately, revenue growth generated by price increases yields higher profits than growth generated by volume increases. The opposite applies in a crisis: A decline in sales volume is less harmful to profit than a decline in price.

In each individual case, the profit effect depends on the variable costs. If the variable costs are zero (such as with standard software), then the profit impact from changes in price and sales volume become identical. The impact that variable and fixed costs has on profit depend on their relative magnitudes. For instance, if we reverse the numbers in our example and set variable costs at $30 and fixed costs at $60 million, the impact on profit from both cost components would be reversed; that is, variable costs would have a profit lever of three and fixed costs would have a profit lever of six.

In many industries the current crisis has caused a considerably greater deterioration of sales volumes, prices, and revenues than the 5

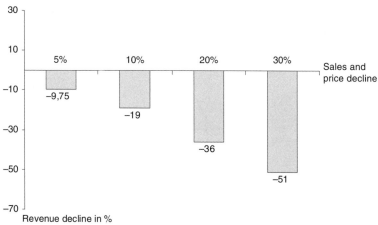

Fig. 2.4: Effect of simultaneous price and sales decline on revenue

or 10% used in our example. And the collapse is not confined to one profit driver. This emphasizes our appeal to utilize all three profit drivers to defend revenues and profits. The greater the crash, the harder it becomes to defend profit with only one driver. In industries where sales volume or revenue have dropped by 30–50%, this is quite simply impossible. The situation becomes much more precarious if prices and sales volumes decline simultaneously. If both decline by 5%, then revenue will decrease by 9.75%. If price and sales volume both drop by 20%, revenue will follow suit with a 36% drop. With a 30% price and sales reduction, revenue plunges by 51%. These combined effects are illustrated in Figure 2.4.

If both price and sales volume collapse – which is often the case in a crisis – the effect on revenue is dramatic, and even more so on profit. As a consequence, efforts to improve all three profit drivers must be stepped up to prevent the ultimate disaster, bankruptcy. Managers' number one duty is to thoroughly understand and quantify the interrelations of these effects in order to avoid making fatal mistakes, such as excessively cutting prices.

The Speed of the Effects

In addition to the magnitude of the sales and profit effects, the speed with which the three profit drivers impact revenue and profitability is of the utmost importance. In Chapter 1, we discussed how managers have been thrown off guard by the suddenness of the drop in revenues

Fig. 2.5: Speed of the effects

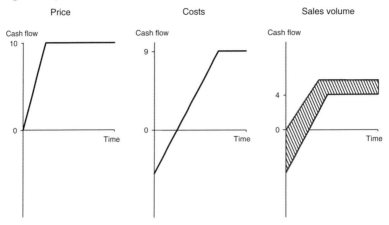

and sales. Any delay in implementing rescue measures can endanger a company's survival. How fast do the profit and cash flow drivers – price, volume, and costs – take effect? Figure 2.5 provides an illustration of the temporal patterns of the cash flow effects. The horizontal axis represents time; the vertical axis shows cash flow.

The speed of implementation and the speed of the effect on cash flow is usually the highest for price. As long as a company is not contractually or legally restricted from raising its prices, it can make price adjustments without delay. The ensuing effect on sales and revenue occurs rather quickly. The case of a gas station depicts this more vividly. The prices can be altered by pressing a computer button, the display registers the change, customers respond accordingly, and the effects on sales volume, revenue, cash flow, and profit are set within hours. Additionally, the costs of the price change are virtually zero in this and many other cases – meaning that no initial investments are required to generate higher profits later on. Of course, the feasibility of such an implementation and the ultimate effects depend on the concrete business model of the individual case. If a company must maintain a price level for a longer period due to contractual obligations, or if a price can only be adjusted when a new catalogue is printed, then the implementation and effect can take considerably longer.

With cost cuts, an upfront investment, which at first leads to negative cash flow, is usually required to achieve a better cost position. For example, layoffs often require severance payments, and other-cost cutting strategies like business process reengineering, organizational restructuring or automation also require significant upfront investment. The problem of upfront investments should not be underestimated. Approximately 80% of all companies in the world are currently working to implement cost-cutting programs. Yet those that are short on cash may prove unable to fully finance their cost-cutting measures. This can cause a true dilemma: while lower costs are crucial for survival, some companies cannot afford the upfront expenses necessary to achieve the savings. The speed of the implementation can be impeded by many factors, such as the existence of labor contracts. The middle part of Figure 2.5 depicts this temporal pattern. Of course, there are cases where an immediate implementation of cost cuts is feasible and the effects occur quickly. For instance, if more favorable buying conditions are negotiated and enacted without delay, the speed of the effect is similar to that of price. In most cases, however, cost cuts require significant upfront investment and achieve the desired savings much later.

As a profit driver, sales volume tends to have a similar temporal pattern as costs. An advertising campaign requires time for preparation and implementation. Any positive effects of the campaign are realized only after a time lag. If you want to ramp up your salesforce, you first need to hire salespeople and train them. This costs time and money without generating an immediate increase in revenue. The new salespeople will only gradually increase sales and revenues. While cash flows are typically negative at first, there are some sales measures that have a more immediate effect without requiring upfront investments or causing initial negative cash flows. One example is the redeployment of office staff to sales. The shaded area in the right part of Figure 2.5 depicts these differentiated patterns.

All solutions that demand little upfront investment and have an immediate positive effect on cash flows are especially suitable for the crisis. Price measures are at the top of this list. Initiatives to cut costs and defend sales are more nuanced. For these two drivers, many quick solutions often cause cash flows to fall initially since they require significant upfront investment and take time to make a positive impact.

A very critical facet of the temporal pattern refers to cash flows. In a crisis, liquidity is more crucial than ever, which is why it is often said that "cash is king." Klaus Kleinfeld, CEO of Alcoa, said in an interview about the crisis that "It's about cash flow, and more cash flow."[6] Profits are absolutely necessary for a company to stay liquid over time. Ultimately, companies must earn more than they spend. In the short term, however, profit and liquidity (i.e., cash flow) are two different things. A profitable company can still go bankrupt, although this is rare. To put it differently: cash flow is like air, and profit is like food.

If you don't get enough air, you will die within minutes. But you can survive without food for several weeks.

Cash flow in a crisis is particularly critical when it comes to managing receivables. On the one hand, the chances of not getting paid are much higher in a crisis than in better economic times. "Our losses from unpaid receivables have increased dramatically," comments Michael Pieper, CEO of Franke Holding.[7] At the same time, it's more difficult to get credit insurance, that is, coverage against losing receivables, during a crisis. Just when vendors have the greatest need for timely payments, many payments end up being delayed by cash-strapped buyers. How a company manages its receivables is crucial during a crisis.

Solutions That Don't Work Against the Crisis

In every crisis, there are always people who claim to have the right remedies. Over and over again we hear hackneyed statements like the following:
"Every crisis offers opportunities – you just have to take advantage of them."
"The innovator will be the winner."
"Those who act courageously now will emerge stronger from the crisis."
"Those who are proactive will emerge victorious."

The following growth strategies are propagated as effective remedies against the crisis:

- Innovation
- Penetration of new markets (new market segments, new countries)
- Diversification
- Acquisition
- Vertical integration
- Radically new business models
- Improving employees' skills

According to a study conducted by a well-known consulting business, "Strong customer orientation, excellent business processes, a flexible organization with good employees and a clear strategy along with a precise definition of the core business" are key success factors during the crisis. Further, a partner from the same consulting firm contends, "In the coming months, there will be more developments that will necessitate a new definition of a company's core business."[8]

Another very popular solution to mitigating the crisis is to increase market share. In a recent report on six companies and how they are coping with the crisis, all six company CEOs were interviewed and all gave the same reply: they want to exploit the current crisis in order to gain market share. For years this has been an all too well-known strategy in the automotive industry, where market share targets of the various contenders always added up to 120 or 130%. We all know how ludicrous this is – the market share sum is and always will be 100 (in good and bad times). The game for market share is zero-sum. Not every company can and will gain market share. For every market share gain there is an equal market share loss. Focusing on increasing market share in the crisis is actually a dangerous goal, with the exception of a few really strong companies. Ultimately, managers should never forget that the survival of their company in the crisis does not depend on market share, but on cash flow and profit.[9]

While all of the above recommendations may indeed be good long-term strategies, in a crisis there are two reasons why they do not function as quick solutions. First, the strategies demand high levels of resources and cash in the immediate short term. Second, they take effect only with a substantial time delay, usually years. As mentioned earlier, what most companies need in the crisis are solutions that can be implemented quickly and generate a significant and positive effect on sales, revenue, cash flow, and profit within a few weeks or months.

A few lucky companies may be able to introduce a newly developed innovation into the market right now. But, if a company starts an innovation project today, a large investment in R&D is required and the innovation now may not be ready to go to market for years. In other words, investing in innovation will not help a company ride out the current crisis. In fact, newly started innovation projects may actually endanger a company's chance of near-term survival. The same applies to the penetration of new foreign markets or market segments. These growth strategies require a high amount of initial investment that pays off only years later. The process of opening new foreign subsidiaries, including finding and training personnel, can take months or even years to complete. In contrast to this, a quick and cost-effective market entry process, such as increasing exports via an importer or distributor, can generate instant additional revenue. A recent study conducted by Simon-Kucher & Partners revealed that during the crisis, companies have a preference for exporting to new markets instead of establishing their own subsidiaries in these target markets.[10]

This time- and cost-saving tactic makes more sense under the current circumstances.

The same applies to radical new business models and projects that aim to increase diversification or vertical integration. Such strategies require companies to move into new business fields that demand competence, market development, and considerable upfront costs and time. Acquisitions are likewise a poor solution to overcoming the immediate problems induced by the crisis. The core business often suffers because of management's pre-occupation with post-merger integration. A lower-scale alternative tactic to buying an entire company is to poach individual employees or teams from weakened competitors (e.g., in sales). When a company begins to weaken, the best employees often start to actively search for a new employer. The crisis creates an auspicious time for companies to hire their weaker competitors' best talents.

Improving employees' skills with additional training seems like a good idea during the crisis, as employees have more time for personal development. Realistically though, increased training translates into increased costs and only provides for longer-term improvements. For these reasons, budgets for continuing education and employee development are usually the first to get cut in a crisis. If the training can be provided without additional costs, for example, when underutilized employees act as trainers, it can be very useful.

The main point is that traditional growth strategies are poorly suited for driving a quick and positive impact during the crisis. And quick, positive effects are exactly what most companies need. In terms of longer-term strategies, the traditional approaches may in fact be useful and effective. For example, acquisitions can be made for bargain prices in difficult times. Companies that are operationally and financially stable can take advantage of the unique opportunities a crisis presents. Nevertheless, even strong companies must maintain a focus on their core businesses so that nothing goes wrong. In a crisis, managers' full attention must be on efficiently steering their companies through the turmoil. This book deals with issues and actions that companies must consider and employ in the immediate future. Facing imminent dangers and impending risks, companies must put traditional long-term growth strategies on the backseat and go after quick wins.

During the crisis, companies should consistently direct the quick solutions they choose towards maximizing profit and cash flow in the short term. They must avoid the temptation of mixing confusing quick solutions with longer-term goals. Every third company is fighting for its survival in the current crisis.[11] And this is what we are talking about here: survival, nothing more and nothing less.

Summary

In the crisis, the implementation, the impact and speed of a solution's effects are critical. All quick solutions must be analyzed taking the aspects discussed in this chapter into consideration. Here are the key points:

- In light of the severity of the declines in revenue and sales, companies must employ all profit drivers to get through the crisis. The necessary improvements cannot be achieved with one profit driver alone.
- The profit drivers have very different effects on profits. Price has by far the strongest profit lever. In contrast, sales volume has a much weaker effect on profit.
- Consequently, it is better to accept a sales decline than a price cut.
- The combination of a sales decline and a price decline marks the worst case scenario and must be avoided at all costs.
- Combined variable and fixed costs have about the same impact on profit that price has by itself. Thus, cost and price improvements are equally important in the crisis. Contrary to this assertion, most executives instinctively focus primarily on cost cutting in the crisis.
- The above statements apply to typical products and their cost structures. The concrete effects are dependent on the specific parameter constellation. This implies that a thorough analysis of the profit drivers and their effects is required in each case.
- The temporal patterns of the profit drivers show marked differences with regard to implementation, upfront costs, and effects.
- Price can typically be adjusted quickly and generates instant effects. The upfront costs of implementing pricing measures are usually negligible.
- Cost cuts frequently take effect only after a long period of time and usually require initial investments that put a strain on cash flow.
- With the profit driver sales volume, the timing of the effects and the costs are strongly dependent on the specific situation.
- Cash flow, or liquidity, takes on the most critical role in the crisis.
- Solutions that target long-term improvements in both strategic market position and growth are poorly suited to fight the crisis. These include innovation, market penetration, acquisitions, diversification, vertical integration, radically new business models, and upgraded training programs. These growth strategies will initially

cause a negative cash flow and undoubtedly exacerbate the challenging financial situation most companies face. Furthermore, the solutions only have a positive impact on cash after several years.

- This does not mean that unique opportunities (like the bargain acquisition of a competitor) should not be exploited when they present themselves. But companies must be careful that they don't overstep their financial strength and become distracted from their core business.
- Looking at the seriousness of the crisis, companies should not pursue too many goals at once. In a crisis, a company must focus on survival – that is, generating and defending sales, revenue, profit, and cash flow. All attention must be directed towards the profit drivers and their effects.

Careful evaluation of the quick solutions must be done. Standard procedures from good times can lead in the wrong direction. Which solutions work during the crisis? How quickly can they be implemented? How fast do they take effect? These are the critical questions.

Endnotes

1 International Monetary Fund, April 2009.
2 For a deeper analysis of the profit drivers see Robert J. Dolan and Hermann Simon, *Power Pricing: How Managing Price Transforms the Bottom Line*, New York: The Free Press 1996, and Hermann Simon and Martin Fassnacht, Preismanagement, Wiesbaden: Gabler 2009.
3 The lever could also be designated as the "profit elasticity of price," because as in each elasticity definition 2% changes are related to each other.
4 See e.g. "Score Upbeat on Rising Premiums," ft.com, March 5, 2009, "Has Equity-Spotting Strategy Changed?" ft.com, January 15, 2009.
5 See Hermann Simon, Frank Bilstein, Frank Luby, *Manage for Profit, Not for Market Share*, Boston: Harvard Business School Press 2006.
6 "Es geht um Liquidität und nochmals Liquidität," interview with Alcoa-CEO Klaus Kleinfeld, *Frankfurter Allgemeine Zeitung*, March 3, 2009, p. 14.
7 "Kampf der Krise," *Bilanz*, February 2009, pp. 24–34.
8 See "From Buy, Buy, to Bye-Bye," economist.com, April 2, 2009, and Julia Leendertse, "Die Krisenstrategien der Wachstumschampions," Wirtschaftswoche online, January 7, 2009.
9 See Hermann Simon, Frank Bilstein und Frank Luby, *Manage for Profit, Not for Market Share*, Boston: Harvard Business School Press 2006.
10 See Philip Grothe und Grigori Bokeria, "Internationale Wachstumsstudie: Strategien und Herausforderungen für Industrieunternehmen – Schock oder Wachstum trotz Krise?", Study by Simon-Kucher & Partners, January 2009.
11 "Jedes dritte Unternehmen bangt ums Überleben," *Frankfurter Allgemeine Zeitung*, March 9, 2009, p. 14.

Chapter 3

Intelligent Cost Cutting

Faced with the catastrophic collapse in revenue, cutting costs has to be the top priority for companies trying to survive the crisis. Cost cutting is inevitable and mandatory in this situation. The challenge is to lower costs quickly without causing any long-term damage to the company. This calls for more intelligent solutions than simple-minded mass layoffs. Companies must utilize as many levers as possible to reduce costs while simultaneously being cautious not to cut back in the wrong places.

Understanding Cost Drivers

In recent years, companies have been rationalizing work and streamlining their operations. Lowering costs (or, to put it the other way, increasing productivity) is an ongoing management responsibility. As a matter of fact, much has been achieved in productivity improvements in recent years. All over the world data shows that productivity has been steadily increasing year after year. The net result is that unit labor costs have dropped. In a discussion with the author a top manager of a leading car maker said, "It is our policy to avoid layoffs, but our productivity grows every year by 5%. This just means that every year we have to sell 5% more cars." To manufacture the same number of cars, the company would therefore need 5% fewer employees every year. In other words, if the sales figures stayed the same, layoffs or reductions of work time would be inevitable.

The situation only worsens if sales figures crash by 10, 20 or 40% – as has been the case in this crisis. Such a dramatic drop in sales makes quick and decisive cost cuts unavoidable. Cost management becomes the number one priority in a recession, and most companies responded accordingly when the crisis hit them. The first measures

H. Simon, *Beat the Crisis: 33 Quick Solutions for Your Company*,
DOI 10.1007/978-1-4419-0823-0_3, © Hermann Simon 2010

were already introduced in the early phase of the crisis. Temporary employees were the first to experience the crunch. Many companies used Christmas and the turn of the year 2008/2009 to extend corporate vacation periods. These measures had a dual purpose: they alleviated volume and margin pressure in the market, and partial pay cuts generated real cost savings. Work time accounts where workers accumulated overtime in prosperous times were offset against unpaid free time. Many companies went a step further and slashed working hours. These are astute and relatively "soft" solutions, but they can only be sustained for a limited period of time. If the crisis continues for a long period, mass layoffs become the only alternative. This is exactly what has happened in the current crisis: in many industries, layoffs and closures have been unavoidable.

The presumed duration of the crisis is a highly critical aspect of all cost considerations. Instant and radical actions like closures and layoffs often seem like a good idea at the moment, but in the long term they may prove to be grave mistakes. Uncertainty runs high, and companies do not know how to react. In this situation it is advisable to make cost adjustments as flexible as possible and to avoid decisions that are difficult to reverse. Instead, companies should use as many cost drivers as possible to achieve the necessary savings.

To illustrate the possibilities, we will do a few simple calculations, looking back at our numerical case from Chapter 1. The price was at $100, the variable unit costs were at $60, and the fixed costs at $30 million. One million product units were sold, putting the revenue at $100 million and the profit at $10 million. What is the breakeven volume, that is, the volume of zero profit, in this case? It is easily determined by dividing the fixed costs by the unit contribution margin (price minus variable unit costs, that is, $100 - 60 = \$40$). $30 million divided by $40 equals 750,000 units. The situation is shown in Figure 3.1.

We now assume that the sales volume in the crisis drops by 40% to 600,000. This figure is clearly below the breakeven volume. Everything else is unchanged. Therefore, revenue sinks to $60 million. Costs fall only to $66 million ($30 million fixed costs plus $600,000 \times 60 = \$36$ million variable costs), thus causing a loss of $6 million. The margin or return on sales is still 10%, but with the wrong (negative) sign. If things continue this way, the company's survival is endangered. Many companies are currently in this situation; that is, their sales and order volumes are far below the breakeven volume.

It is obvious that costs and the breakeven volume have to be reduced considerably and quickly. If the company in our case could

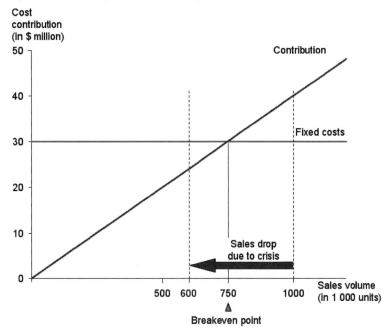

Fig. 3.1: Sales drop and breakeven point

effectively lower the variable unit costs by 20% to $48, the unit contribution margin would reach $52 and the breakeven volume would drop to 576,923 units. As a result, a sales volume of 600,000 units would be above the breakeven volume – even achieving a modest profit of $1.2 million or 2% of sales. Decreasing the variable costs by 15%, on the other hand, would not put the company in the profit zone. There would still be a loss of $600,000.

Lowering the fixed costs by 20%, normally impossible in the short term, leads to a breakeven volume of 600,000 units and, thus, zero profit. If the fixed costs go down by 10% – a big achievement – the breakeven point would be at 675,000 units. In this case, the 40% sales decline still causes a loss of $3 million and endangers survival.

A 40% sales decline in the current crisis is not common, but it's also not unrealistic. Some industries experience even more severe sales crashes. Our simple calculations reveal that extreme cost cuts are necessary to compensate for such collapses. A short-term drop of 10, 15, let alone 20%, in variable unit costs is difficult to achieve. This is even truer for fixed costs, which by definition do not vary by volume and cannot be reduced quickly. Cost cuts alone are simply not sufficient to counter the dramatic sales and revenue drops in the current crisis.

Companies must mobilize all available forces on the sales and price fronts to alleviate the sales collapse.

Our case demonstrates the influence of various cost parameters and combinations thereof. Steep variable costs are an advantage in a crisis, while flat variable costs are better in growth periods. In our example, a $60 variable unit cost is fairly high and the cost curve is thus steep. In the context of a dramatic sales drop, this means that total costs plunge dramatically. With a sales decline of 40% or 400,000 units, variable costs automatically slide by $24 million. If we flip the figures around, that is, assume fixed costs of $60 million and variable unit costs of $30, the initial situation would not change. Revenue would remain at $100 million, total costs at $90 million, and profit at $10 million. The breakeven volume would, however, strongly increase to 857,143 units from 750,000 units ($60 million divided by $70). A sales collapse of 40% would cause variable costs to decline by only $12 million and cause a loss of $18 million. The negative margin or return on sales (ROS) shoots up to a menacing 30% – enough to quickly take a company down. In times of growth, we see the opposite effect. If sales volume climbs to 1.2 million units from 1 million, $18 million in profit would result in the original cost parameters ($60 variable unit costs and $30 million fixed costs). This profit would be 80% higher than what we started with. In a situation with $60 million fixed costs and $30 variable unit costs, profit jumps 140% to $24 million. When a company grows, flat variable costs are favorable; in a crisis, it's better to have steep variable costs.

A similar situation is well known: a firm choosing between an employed sales rep or an independent (self-employed) agent. If revenue is low, agents are more affordable as they earn only commissions (variable costs), but do not incur any fixed costs. In contrast, it is cheaper to employ the sales rep in times of high or increasing revenue, as they receive a fixed pay (fixed costs), but take in only small commissions (variable costs). In other words, companies with high shares of variable costs have an advantage in the current crisis.

Apply Multiple Cost Parameters

Every cost category must be carefully examined during the crisis. As this book focuses on programs for defending revenue and profits, we will not delve deeply into all cost types and cost-cutting options, but refer instead to special literature.[1] In any case, it is important to remain realistic about cost-cutting potential in view of the extreme slumps in sales and revenue. Cost-cutting potentials are often quite limited today. In recent years, purchase prices have been pushed down to an extent that the scope for further cuts is now constrained. Manufacturing and supply chain processes have been optimized so that the room for further improvement is quite narrow. In addition, improvements here will require major investments, for example, in automation, which are unrealistic during the crisis.

Companies seriously hit by the crisis can hardly avoid cutting back on their labor costs. Ultimately, cutting back on labor costs is the only way of achieving cost reductions that are large enough to cope with the decline in volumes. We will therefore now turn to various intelligent options for labor cost reductions. Many companies are being forced to implement mass layoffs or fully close down operations. In 2009, America has the highest unemployment rate in the last 25 years.[2]

But there are various ways of lowering personnel costs before such drastic measures as mass layoffs or plant closures have to be taken. The relevant cost drivers include the following:

- Number of employees
- Hourly wages
- Hours worked per day
- Days worked per week

Vacation days, special leave, different wage brackets, and so on can be added to this list. We will restrict ourselves to a simple example here. Let us assume that the company under consideration had a weekly wage budget of $10 million before the crisis set in. From this budget it paid 10,000 employees who earn $25 an hour, worked 8 h a day, and 5 days a week ($10,000 \times \$25 \times 8 \times 5 = \$10$ million). In the crisis revenue falls by 20%. We assume that the weekly wage budget drops by the same percentage to $8 million. What can the company do? Taking one parameter at a time, it can:

- Lay off 2,000 employees or
- Cut the hourly wage to $20 or
- Reduce the daily work time to 6.4 hours or
- Introduce a 4-day work week

Leaving aside the political feasibility of these measures, we can see that by simply using one cost driver there are already numerous options for reducing labor costs. From a social point of view, however, the appropriateness of each option differs widely.

The outcome of a combined package of measures is even more revealing. Figure 3.2 shows the discussed scenarios in which only one cost driver is reduced as well as various combinations of cost drivers (A, B and C). All these variants cut the labor costs to less than $8 million.

Combining cost drivers appears less drastic than simply making "one-dimensional" mass layoffs. Further cost drivers can be included, such as wage adjustments for individual employees or employee groups, unpaid vacation, special leave with part pay, part-time work models, and so on. Another method is to slow down the speed of assembly lines, as some automotive manufacturers are doing.

So far, our examination of cost-cutting measures has assumed a 20% drop in revenue and ensuingly in the wage budget. The situation looks much better if we assume that the company is fighting against the sales slump and can limit the revenue decline to 10%. Then the wage budget only has to be cut by 10% instead of 20%. Combination D (the bottom row in Figure 3.2) shows that the necessary cuts in this case are considerably less drastic than in the 20% cost reduction scenario. Now each cost driver only has to be lowered by a small amount and the hourly wage is not even touched. These kinds of "softer" solutions make a lot of sense. Even so, employees will have to face the bitter truth that pay cuts are inevitable.

Is it possible to adopt these flexible solutions in practice? Today we answer this question more optimistically than we did 10 years ago. Many of the options outlined above have been implemented during the current crisis. Employers and trade unions have recognized the gravity of the situation and are willing to make significant concessions and act more flexibly. This behavior is not entirely new. Labor conditions

Fig. 3.2: Cutting costs by combining various cost drivers

Alternatives	Number of Employees	Hourly Wage ($)	Working Hours per Day	Working Days per Week	Total Wage Costs ($)
Before	10,000	25	8	5	10,000,000
Only Layoffs	8,000	25	8	5	8,000,000
Wage Cuts	10,000	20	8	5	8,000,000
6.4-hour Days	10,000	25	6.4	5	8,000,000
4-day Weeks	10,000	25	8	4	8,000,000
Combination A	9,000	22.2	8	5	7,992,000
Combination B	9,600	24	7.2	4.8	7,962,624
Combination C	10,000	25	7	4.5	7,875,000
Combination D*	9,750	25	7.5	4.9	8,957,813

* The slump in total revenue and wages was limited to 10% thanks to revenue-boosting measures.

have long become more flexible, especially at midsized companies. Managers in many markets face the constant challenge of balancing rigid resources against fluctuating market demands, whether there is a crisis or not. The rigidity of resources is partly due to government regulations such as dismissal protection and other rules that constrain a company's maneuverability (concerning relocations, reassignments, wage adjustments and so on). But many of the restricting factors (such as wage and bargaining agreements, company policy and corporate culture) reside in the companies themselves. Our study of hidden champions revealed that many of these midsized market leaders are much more flexible than large corporations.

Claas, a leading manufacturer of harvesting machines, whose business is highly seasonal, has a long-established model of weekly work time that can vary between 24 and 51 hours, without additional pay. Employees at Wacker Neuson, which builds construction machinery, work up to 48 hours a week at peak times. Hidden champions such as Trumpf and Hermle spearheaded the introduction of flexible work-time accounts and have been using them for many years.[3] The models adopted by Volkswagen in times of crisis also demonstrate that employees are increasingly accepting more flexible solutions. This attitude of workers and their organizations is vital for tackling the current crisis. Combined approaches (such as shown in Figure 3.2) will be more effective than a one-dimensional approach, and will be more widely accepted. But these ideas cannot be turned into reality unless everyone involved climbs down from dogmatic positions and pulls together as a team.

The willingness to accept such flexible schemes and the actual applications differs strongly across countries. According to Franz Fehrenbach, CEO of Bosch, the world's largest automotive supplier with over $50 billion in revenue, "Germany has become an international role model with its instruments for making work time more flexible."[4] Fehrenbach is in a position to compare since Bosch employs 271,000 people in all major countries in the world. Recently, the author discussed the solutions outlined in Figure 3.2 with French business journalists, whose unanimous response was, "You couldn't do that in France." Relations between employers and unions are too rigid to allow for such flexibility. In Japan, the situation is again different. Employees accept shortened worktimes, but employers that cut working hours still have to pay full wages. Thus, no cost reduction is achieved, an absurd consequence.

The U.S. has one of the most flexible labor markets, and as a result American companies can shed employees relatively easily in a downturn and then rehire when times improve. Such flexibility provides less incentive for U.S. firms to avoid layoffs. This is further compounded by the fact that U.S. firms pick up a large portion of the health insurance bill of their workers due to the lack of social safety nets, and thus can cut costs beyond wages by dismissing employees.

Such flexibility does not mean U.S. companies should not strive to find more creative solutions. In downturns, hours worked decline on average and some firms seek alternatives to dismissals, especially for highly skilled employees. For example, a New York law firm is currently offering one third of base pay to associates to not show up to work for a year.[5] Pella Corp., a large window and door manufacturer, recently ordered 2,400 hourly employees to take rotating weeklong furloughs to avoid layoffs. "We have really good people working for us, and we don't want to lose them," says Karen Peterson, vice president of human resources at Pella.[6] However, according to a recent survey of 245 U.S. companies, layoffs are still more common, with 65% stating they had cut jobs or plan to cut jobs compared to 36% that are ordering or offering furloughs.[7] With the onset of the crisis, companies like CISCO implemented a shutdown around Christmas (a situation they avoided in the Internet downturn in 2001/2002, but could not avoid in this crisis). Many companies in the Silicon Valley where semiconductor and electronics have been hit hard by demand downturns of 20–40% have commonly implemented such measures as mandatory vacations or "shutdown days." Companies shut down their offices every other Friday until demand returns. There have also been substantial layoffs. In the course of 2009 these numbers have been picking up as companies acknowledge that the crisis will likely last well into 2010. Many companies are taking advantage of this crisis to not only remove underperforming employees, but also to reassign and retrain employees across their organizations.

As companies dig in for a longer economic siege, many have taken the opportunity to idle or shut down older plants. Ironically, many cash strapped companies face the situation that they don't have the upfront cash required to close plants and so they have to continue to run them even at a loss. This situation puts companies with a strong cash position at a significant advantage not just because they have better operating reserves, but also because they have more cost-cutting options. Companies with stronger cash positions and less debt (long ridiculed by Wall Street) now find themselves in a strong position to acquire troubled competitors (or at the very least their customers).

Overall, it is surprising that the simple, logical solutions outlined in Figure 3.2 are still regarded as nothing short of revolutionary in many countries.

Take Advantage of Insourcing

Outsourcing, or transferring work to a third-party provider, has become a major trend in recent years. In most cases cost cutting was the motivation to outsource. The third-party provider, often based in a low-wage country, simply offered to make the product or provide the service at a lower cost. As an unwarranted side effect many companies experienced quality problems from outsourcing. It is revealing that market and quality leaders outsource far less than average companies. The hidden champions, for example, have a vertical integration of 42%, that is, 42% of the value added is created internally while the average for industrial companies is only 29.8%.[8]

Insourcing can be a useful way of bringing work back to the company and improving capacity utilization. If the costs of underutilized capacity are mainly fixed, insourcing can result in lower unit costs. This is because the outsourcing costs no longer apply, and internally only the marginal costs have to be added. How quickly these effects emerge depends on contractual obligations. Given sufficient flexibility, a company can outsource more actively during a boom, and revert back to insourcing during a slump. This system works in a way similar to flexible work-time accounts.

One variation of this method is "internal insourcing," that is, relocating production from abroad back to the home market. Bertram Kandziora, CEO of Stihl, the world's leading chainsaw manufacturer, recently announced that production of 100,000 chain saws would be relocated from the U.S. and Brazil to the company's main plant in Germany. As most of the associated costs will be incremental, this decision could result in considerable savings.[9] It will also secure jobs at the parent plant.

Where Not to Save

The tremendous cost pressure exerted by the crisis harbors a major risk of saving at the wrong end. Across-the-board budget cuts are generally regarded as an effective way of implementing unpopular measures. But the danger is that across-the-board cuts can also do away with activities that could help to tackle the crisis. It is indeed challenging to strike the right balance necessary for short-term cost reductions and their long-term consequences.

Given the imminent cost pressures, employee layoffs may seem unavoidable, even within the core workforce. Yes, these layoffs may effectively reduce costs, but they also endanger valuable know-how. Letting experienced people go in a crisis is a big risk. What happens if these qualified workers are needed again in 6 or 9 months but don't come back? They may have become disillusioned with the company and looked for a job elsewhere. Employee turnover and the associated loss of expertise is a factor whose strategic importance can hardly be overestimated, especially for companies with a highly skilled workforce. The hidden champions are an excellent case in point. Their average annual labor turnover rate is just 2.7%, compared with 7.3% for Germany as a whole, and a very high 30.3% for the U.S.[10] Personnel bottlenecks will become more likely in the next economic upturn. In many industrialized countries unfavorable demographics will aggravate these bottlenecks.

Crisis or not, employers should therefore avoid letting go of highly qualified employees, or at least keep the cutbacks to a minimum. Wendelin Wiedeking, CEO of Porsche, is emphatic on this point, "Our people are highly qualified and extremely committed, so we don't take questions about job security lightly."[11] Mark Hurd, CEO of Hewlett-Packard, takes a similar view, "We think that eliminating talent and then quickly rehiring talent is an expensive and risky proposition."[12] Siemens-CEO Peter Loescher joins in, "We want the important know-how of our technicians and engineers to stay within the company."[13] And Franz Fehrenbach, CEO of Bosch, states, "We want to retain our core workforce worldwide for as long as possible."[14] But Jim O'Neill, Head of Global Economic Research at Goldman Sachs, also points to a dilemma facing listed companies, "If the slump turns out to be severe but only short-term, companies that reduce inventory and cut back staff too aggressively will suddenly have to restock and rehire just as aggressively. But for most CEOs, especially those running public companies that risk falling stock prices, it seems easier to cut and take the risk. The equity markets are likely to remain unforgiving of companies that are too optimistic and don't cut costs."[15]

Cuts in R&D budgets are also raising difficult issues. These cuts are comparatively simple to push through, but the long-term effects can be fatal. The lawnmower method is equally inadvisable here. Although cuts are necessary and inevitable, acting hastily and indiscriminately involves great risks. There is no simple solution to this problem. A crisis always poses the threat that long-term investments will suffer due to the intense cost pressure. Craig Barrett, former CEO of Intel, shares his view on the subject, "You cannot save your way out of the recession; you can only invest your way out."[16] Not every company has the financial strength of Intel, but Barrett's advice should be carefully considered.

Savings that may weaken a company's market position should also be approached with great caution. Time and again, we observe that firms counter cost pressure by scrimping on product quality. Such cuts can be extremely harmful, in both the medium and the long term. This is illustrated by automakers' experiences with the radical cutbacks by the infamous Ignacio Lopez who worked for General Motors and later Volkswagen. Even in the crisis, customers are reluctant to accept inferior quality. On the contrary, as we learned in Chapter 1, the crisis leads to a greater emphasis on safety, and good quality plays a vital role. The key is to distinguish between components that impact the customers' quality perception and those that don't. However, this tenet has long since been practiced in the automotive industry and other sectors. Companies are strongly advised not to give in to cost pressures by delivering poorer-quality products.

Another crucial distinction must be made between value-creating activities with an immediate impact and measures that have no, or only a very long-term, effect on results. This applies equally to cost-cutting and sales-promoting activities. In marketing, for example, cutting back on sponsoring or long-term image-boosting measures is more acceptable in the crisis than reducing the budget for activities that have an immediate impact on sales. According to Wendelin Wiedeking, Porsche seeks savings "only in those areas that do not add value or do not have a direct effect on revenue."[17]

A hazard emerges when cost-oriented managers or investors get their hands on companies whose success hinges on "soft" factors such as brand image, customer enthusiasm or reputation. These soft values do not just exist but call for ongoing investments. The returns on these investments usually cannot be quantified in hard numbers. Notorious cost cutters often dismiss the importance of such soft factors. A recent study revealed that budget cuts lead to a loss of market share during a recession.[18] The opposite seems to be also true. Nivea, one of the world's leading personal care brands, increased its advertising budget during the last crisis and gained market share. Based on this experience, Nivea-CEO Thomas B. Quaas plans to keep advertising expenditure high during the current crisis. His prediction: "We will outperform the market."[19] Meanwhile, the U.S. brewery Anheuser-Busch appears to be facing the opposite scenario.

Its marketing budget is to be slashed following its takeover by the Belgian/Brazilian brewing conglomerate InBev, whose management is known to keep a close eye on costs. A recent article stated, "InBev's cost-cutting culture kills the buzz at Anheuser-Busch."[20] The trade-off between marketing needs and cost requirements must always be considered carefully. During a crisis, the danger of making cuts in the wrong places is very great.

The crisis also calls for a discussion on consulting budgets. Some companies take the lawnmower approach here as well, while others are more selective. The complexity of the current problems requires a more broad-minded attitude than simply cutting out consulting projects altogether. Instead, it makes more sense to award projects based on their rapid and tangible profit impact. In consulting, it is relatively easy to distinguish between projects with an immediate effect and longer-term, "nice to have" undertakings.

Summary

Cost cutting has to be the top priority in the crisis. The key is to lower costs intelligently and flexibly, thus minimizing negative long-term repercussions. The main takeaways of this chapter are:

- Economizing and boosting productivity are ongoing management responsibilities. The severity of the crisis makes these tasks even more important, and the necessary cost cuts significantly exceed previous proportions. Many companies will be unable to avoid radical measures such as mass layoffs and factory closures.
- Both the extent and duration of the revenue collapse are very important factors for the introduction of appropriate cost-cutting measures. Uncertainty surrounding the issue is very high. This induces the danger of making serious mistakes.
- A trivial point, but one that should still be mentioned and kept in mind, is that steep cost curves (i.e., high variable unit costs) are advantageous in the crisis. High fixed costs, on the other hand, can be fatal. The leverage effect works ruthlessly in the crisis.
- Instead of cutting labor costs by tackling only one cost driver (i.e., layoffs), employers should combine as many cost drivers as possible into a flexible model. This enables savings that are not only more socially acceptable, but also less harmful in the long term from a strategic perspective.
- Flexible labor approaches require that employers, employees, and their unions are willing to cooperate undogmatically. Examples

from midsized companies and some large corporations show that acceptance of creative solutions is growing.
- Companies must be careful not to cut in the wrong places. The across-the-board method may be effective with regard to implementation, but the risk of doing away with valuable activities is high. Selective approaches are superior, even in the crisis.
- Balancing short-term benefits and long-term effects remains difficult.
- It is generally inadvisable to cut back on expenditures that have a quick and quantifiable impact on profits.

Cost cutting is the most common tool for tackling the crisis, not least because it is ostensibly under companies' control – unlike market measures, in which the customers also have a say. However, even on the cost side control is not complete. Cutbacks always affect people, be it employees or suppliers. That's why it is important not to go too far, otherwise the reactions on the other side could be disastrous.

Endnotes

1 Concerning general cost-cutting measures, see. David W. Young, *A Manager's Guide to Creative Cost Cutting: 101 Ways to Build the Bottom Line*, New York: McGraw-Hill 2002, and Andrew Wileman, *Driving Down Cost: How to Manage and Cut Costs Intelligently*, London: Nicholas Brealey Publishing 2008. On short-time work, see: Friedhelm Nyhuis, "Krisenpille Kurzarbeit – So wird sie richtig angewendet," *Produktion*, January 29, 2009, p. 10.
2 "When Jobs Disappear," economist.com, March 12, 2009.
3 Hermann Simon, *Hidden Champions of the 21st Century*, New York: Springer 2009.
4 "Die Kurzarbeit ist ein teures Werkzeug," Interview with Franz Fehrenbach, CEO of Robert Bosch, *Frankfurter Allgemeine Zeitung*, March 14, 2009, p. 16.
5 Susan Dominus, "$80,000 for a Year Off? She'll Take It!" *The New York Times*, April 12, 2009, p. A1.
6 Cari Tuna, "Weighing Furloughs vs. Layoff," *The Wall Street Journal*, April 13, 2009, p. B6.
7 Ibid.
8 Hermann Simon, *Hidden Champions of the 21st Century*, New York: Springer 2009.
9 "Motorsägenhersteller Stihl braucht neue Mitarbeiter," Wirtschaftsblatt.at, December 20, 2008.
10 Hermann Simon, *Hidden Champions of the 21st Century*, New York: Springer 2009.
11 "Sportwagenhersteller Porsche muss sparen," *Frankfurter Allgemeine Zeitung*, January 31, 2009, p. 14.
12 "Mark Hurd's Moment," *Fortune*, March 16, 2009, p. 51.

13 Martin Noé, Thomas Werres, "Führen statt klagen," *Manager Magazin*, March 2009, p. 38.

14 "Die Kurzarbeit ist ein teures Werkzeug," Interview with Franz Fehrenbach, CEO Robert Bosch, *Frankfurter Allgemeine Zeitung*, March 14, 2009, p. 16.

15 "Gaze Into the Crystal Ball," *Newsweek*, February 9, 2009, p. 48.

16 "A Perfect Time to Invest," *Newsweek*, February 9, 2009, p. 48.

17 "Porsche muss sparen," *Der Tagesspiegel*, January 31, 2009, p. 15.

18 Michael Reidel, "Rezepte in der Rezession," *Horizont*, March 5, 2009, p. 4.

19 Ibid.

20 "Belt-Tightening at the House of Bud," *Fortune*, March 16, 2009, p. 10.

Chapter 4

Quick Solutions for Changing Customer Needs

In Chapter 1 we analyzed how customer behavior changes in a period of crisis. More than anything else, their perception of risk increases and their risk tolerance falls. This statement applies equally to consumers and to B2B customers. Consumers are apprehensive about the future and begin to hoard cash. Business customers are reluctant to make investments and long-term commitments. In this particular crisis, the difficulties in getting credit also constrain purchasing power.

In thinking about these changes in both risk perception and risk tolerance, suppliers face the question of whether they can offer their customers deals which appear less risky and thus can overcome their customers' reluctance to buy. Such deals by nature force the supplier to bear greater risk. Suppliers need to examine very carefully how much it will cost them to take on this increased risk and whether these costs put their own firm in danger. Differences can exist, though, between the risks the customer perceives and the objective burden the supplier would face, which means certain forms of risk sharing can be advantageous for both parties.

Quick Solution 1: Offer Extended Warranties

A direct and effective way to reduce risks perceived by customers is to provide guarantees or warranties, which transfer some risk from the customer to the supplier. In early 2009, a developer had 343 vacation homes under construction. Sales became increasingly slow with the ongoing crisis. Even though construction was well underway, the firm had sold only 60 units. The unexpectedly low cash flow endangered the developer of the park. In that situation the developer decided to offer buyers a guaranteed return on the rent of the vacation homes – this response was intended to overcome the fears and

H. Simon, *Beat the Crisis: 33 Quick Solutions for Your Company*,
DOI 10.1007/978-1-4419-0823-0_4, © Hermann Simon 2010

reservations among potential buyers.[1] First responses indicate that this guarantee works.

The U.S. software firm Infusionsoft offers a money-back guarantee if customers do not double their sales within one year through the use of Infusionsoft's sales software. The software is designed specifically for firms with less than ten employees. The guarantee is tied to the actual use of the software, that is, data input and updating on a regular basis. The price for the software is roughly $4,000, which will be refunded if the sales increase is not met. Infusionsoft claims that this guarantee has led to a massive reduction in customers' resistance to buy. Even customers who don't achieve the 100% sales increase in the first year usually keep the software.[2]

Ficion Audio, an American dealer for premium audio equipment, saw demand for its high-end speakers plummet. This equipment normally sells for between $3,400 and $15,000. Ficion offered its customers relief in case of job loss. If a customer loses his or her job within one year after the purchase, 90% of the purchase price will be reimbursed. If the job loss occurs between one and two years after purchase, the customer can return the product and gets 75% of the purchase price back.[3]

The most discussed guarantee is undoubtedly the Hyundai Assurance Program. Hyundai has launched an advertising campaign in the U.S. where it promises "certainty in uncertain times."[4] If a customer finances or leases a car but loses his or her job and thus no longer has a source of income, the customer can return the car without any obligation to make future payments. Hyundai even absorbs negative equity in the car (the difference between what is owed and what the car is worth) up to $7,500. This campaign receives much of the credit for Hyundai's ability to buck the downward trend in automotive sales in 2009. While nearly all competitors saw year-on-year declines – many of them 30–40% – Hyundai has achieved double-digit increases in sales. The Korean firm has since modified the campaign. Now it will pay a customer's monthly payment for three months in order to give the customer the opportunity to find a job. If after three months the customer still has no regular source of income, he or she can still return the car. In other countries one finds similar offers from insurance companies. In case of job loss the premium is covered by the insurance policy for a certain period of time.

In order to find the optimal allocation of risk from the supplier's point of view, a supplier first needs to know how customers perceive risks and respond to uncertainty. Do risk perception and risk aversion form a barrier to buying? Or is that not the case? If the risk barrier exists, how can the supplier overcome it? Second, the supplier must thoroughly understand its own risks during the crisis. Finally, the supplier should make sure to underwrite risks in such a way that its exposure is contained should a customer become insolvent.

Quick Solution 2: Arrange Trial Periods for Machines

Many manufacturing sectors have experienced sharp declines in demand. Accordingly, the customers have become very reluctant to invest in new machinery, even when the new machines would be much more productive than the equipment they are currently using. Buying a machine or committing to a long-term lease agreement means a considerable financial obligation for a manufacturer, and thus creates risk. How can the vendor of the machine alleviate or offset these perceived risks? One simple way is to allow the customer to operate the new machine on a trial or month-to-month basis. In contrast to a purchase or a standard leasing arrangement, which may last for five years, the customer incurs no long-term obligations. The customer can end the agreement and return the equipment at any time. The customer pays a monthly rent, which is higher than the standard leasing rate, but incurs no long-term contractual obligations. Naturally, the machinery vendor bears a much greater risk during this "trial period," in the same way that real estate developers or landlords do when they offer short-term or month-to-month leases to tenants.

Nomis Precision,[5] a manufacturer of machine tools, had a make-to-stock production system and a large number of unsold machines in stock. Putting these machines to use in a "trial" program made more sense than holding them back in the hope that better times will come soon. First, the machines deployed in this program immediately generated incremental revenue. Second, inventories declined, which had a positive effect on company morale. Many customers actually retained the machines because they learned how productive they were relative to existing equipment.

Consumer goods makers can also employ this quick solution. TASSIMO, a fully automated coffee machine from Kraft Foods, is offered for a risk-free trial period of six weeks. The consumer buys the machine as usual, but has the option to return it for a full refund, even if the machine has been used extensively during the trial period.

Quick Solution 3: Accept Success-Dependent Payments

Success- or performance-based payments shift risk from the customer to the supplier because the payments are based on the customer's success. One commonly finds these deals in long-term lease agreements for facilities such as hotels. The hotel operator pays a fixed rent plus an additional amount, which depends on the hotel's revenues or profits. This reduces the operator's risk compared to a lease agreement with one (higher) fixed rate. In contrast, the property's owner bears a greater risk, but also has an upside if the property is particularly successful.

Enercon, the global technology leader for wind turbines, offers its customers this kind of arrangement.[6] In the Enercon Partner Concept (EPC) the price of the contract for maintenance, security, and repairs depends on the returns from the wind farm. Enercon thus shares the commercial risk with the operator of the wind farm, thereby considerably reducing the operator's risk. Customers seem to find this setup appealing, because 85% of them sign up for the EPC-contract.

Like all other assumptions of risks or guarantees, a supplier has to take the costs into account. But these have remained manageable for Enercon because of the quality of its products. Enercon is the only large manufacturer whose wind turbines do not have gears. Installations with gears tend to break down more often and require more maintenance. Due to its gearless equipment Enercon can guarantee an uptime of 97% and actually achieves 99% on average. Thus, the guaranteed uptime of 97% effectively doesn't cost Enercon anything. All in all, this represents a best practice in the optimal sharing of risk between a customer and the supplier and allows Enercon to overcome customers' reluctance to sign long-term service contracts.

Quick Solution 4: Communicate Tangible Benefits

In Chapter 1, we outlined that two phenomena that emerge in a deep crisis like the current one: price elasticities evolve unfavorably and customers pay higher attention to tangible, visible benefits and costs. If these assumptions are true, they have consequences for how to communicate with customers in a crisis. It is evident that in order to achieve certain volume targets in a crisis, deeper price cuts than usual are necessary – and these price cuts have to be communicated more strongly than in normal times. Discount retail chains follow this practice to stress the "value for price" they offer. In many countries we see much stronger advertising by discounters during the crisis. This seems strange but it indicates that an intensified price communication is necessary to overcome the reduced price elasticity.

But "value for price" should not be a synonym for "dirt cheap." In the crisis companies should shift their communication away from the typical softer image-oriented messages and toward the focused communication of specific tangible benefits and cost-benefit advantages. Crisis aside, B2B suppliers should practice this kind of communication as a matter of course. The crisis only makes this more important. A company can also emphasize short-term advantages as customers think more about what they need and can afford right now versus advantages that may take longer to realize.

This stronger orientation towards tangible benefits definitely applies to consumers. If car buyers increasingly concern themselves with measurable facts such as gas mileage, emissions, and a car's resale value, manufacturers need to stress advantages in these attributes in their advertising. The same applies to car parts and products. The advertising for the popular anti-freeze Prestone reflected this new direction last winter. The television ad shows one customer apparently selecting a lower-priced product until another customer intervenes. This other customer explains that, yes, one might save a few dollars right now, but who can afford to get stuck nowadays with a car that won't start? That would be much more expensive. Why take that risk by buying the less expensive product rather than Prestone? Such a redirection of a company's advertising assumes, of course, that it can demonstrate the tangible advantages. And the company has to be sure that the crisis has actually altered its customers' perceptions and preferences.

Quick Solution 5: Capitalize on Your Financial Strength

One of the most severe consequences of the crisis is much tighter credit. Financial institutions demand better credit ratings and have become very cautious in making loans. This has hit private and corporate lending in a similar way. This means that a significant amount of demand dries up, as customers who want to buy can't finance their purchase and need to pull back. The crisis also means that longer-term loans will remain few and far between. For suppliers who have sufficient financial resources, however, the crisis presents a unique opportunity to use that strength to their advantage.

The Enercon Partner Concept (EPC) mentioned earlier addresses this problem. Enercon assumes half the service fees for the first six years of the 12-year-contract. Wind farm investors usually are under greatest financial pressure in the first years following the investment. The deal with Enercon offers a wind farm operator significant financial relief during these critical years.

Other companies offer to take payment in installments. The manager of a large trade fair operator said that "In spite of the crisis we will not undermine the value of the services we provide by making price cuts. But we are willing to discuss alternative payment plans, installment payments, or the inclusion of additional services."[7]

The Jordan's Furniture chain, part of Warren Buffett's Berkshire Hathaway empire, uses both its financial strength and the appeal of sports to its advantage. For several years it has offered customers who make a big-ticket purchase the full amount of their purchase back if the local baseball team, the Boston Red Sox, wins the World Series in a sweep; that is, the Red Sox win the best-of-seven series in only four games. The Red Sox did exactly that in 2004, when they won the World Series for the first time in 86 years. They repeated that performance with another sweep in 2007. Jordan's has used insurance to offset the financial risk of this program. The crisis has led Jordan's to amend the offer for 2009. If the Red Sox sweep, the customer still gets furniture for free. But no matter what, the customer receives a gift certificate valid for 20% off of an additional purchase in 2009. Jordan's hopes that the additional incentive will help bring in customers who would have otherwise deferred the purchase of a new bedroom or living room suite.

The extent to which customers appreciate help with financing in tough times is particularly noticeable in Russia, which experienced a very serious economic crisis ten years ago. During that time, German machinery companies offered their Russian customers financing plans that were more flexible and generous than those of competitors from other countries. Even today, ten years later, Russian entrepreneurs told the author how much they appreciated the financial support and they haven't forgotten. Helping customers in difficult times can be a very effective and long-lasting way to build loyalty.

Financing bottlenecks are often particularly severe in growth markets with high latent demand. Markets for alternative energies offer again an illustrative case. "Green" power generation (wind, solar, geo-thermic, etc.) requires huge upfront investments that the investors can rarely finance themselves. "The green energy movement's over-whelming reliance on credit may be its downfall in the current cri-sis," one observer noted.[8] A supplier of green energy technology thus has an enormous competitive advantage if it can support its customers with generous financing plans.

Attractive financing can also boost consumer demand. Currently, many car companies offer free financing for months or even years, and some retailers, such as Best Buy, advertise similar plans for big-ticket items such as appliances or furniture, or an aggregate purchase that crosses a certain threshold. In Europe, these thresholds can be as low as 150 Euros, or less than $200. For many consumers facing tighter credit, the prospect of alternative financing has proven to be more attractive than a rebate or "cash back" offer of identical value. Let's take the example of a flat-screen TV for $2,000 and assume financing for one year costs the seller $150. The dealer could alternatively offer the customer the $150 straight up as a discount. But in that case, the customer must still pay $1,850 upfront. In the former case, the customer makes no payments for a year. That can be a much more compelling offer for a financially stressed consumer during the crisis, even though he may eventually end up paying the same amount.

It is obvious that sellers making these kinds of offers face tremendous risks if they draw in the wrong customers. The success of such programs depends heavily on the ability to select and vet the right customers. Only financially sound companies can consider this strategy because of these risks. But even in those cases, a manufacturer should carefully consider and estimate the risks and reflect them in the prices they charge.

Quick Solution 6: Accept Barter Trades

If a customer has financial problems and can't pay in cash, that cus-tomer may nonetheless have a product, service or asset of value to the supplier. This creates an opportunity for a barter transaction. This archaic transaction model always comes back in difficult times. An eco-nomic crisis can lead customers and suppliers to slip back into more archaic forms of economic interaction. This was the case for decades with cash-strapped developing countries. In exchange for shipments of machinery, chemicals or pesticides, suppliers would get money, but had to accept commodities such as rice or wood. Barter transactions have continued to play an important role in many countries even after the fall of the Iron Curtain.

An advertising agency working for a famous, but financially stressed, sports franchise accepted such a barter agreement. The franchise was not able to pay the full price quoted by the agency for its services in 2009 but offered the use of one of the stadium's VIP suites. The agency accepted the deal because it saw a clear business value in this offer. It invited its key customers to attend games in style. The agency's willingness to accept a barter deal helped it win the contract. The sports franchise got the service and the agency fostered its business development efforts in a way that it considered effective – a "win–win" – outcome for both business partners. Why shouldn't a machinery manufacturer that needs new trucks consider delivering new machines to a truck manufacturer, who would in turn pay with trucks that it currently cannot sell on the open market? This is just one of many barter deals that would represent a "win–win" for both sides.

Quick Solution 7: Lure Customers Away from Weakened Competitors

The crisis can affect individual companies in the same industry in very different ways. The differences among banks in the current crisis are particularly striking. Significant differences have begun to emerge in other industries as well. Highly leveraged companies are vulnerable and quickly come under pressure from creditors. In some markets marginal players who survived in good times will likewise face potential failure in an economic crisis.

A supplier's bankruptcy – or even just the prospect of it – will cause an increasing number of customers to start looking elsewhere for purchasing products or services. Rumors are often sufficient to ignite this process. Sometimes the customer has strong objective reasons to consider switching. It is clearly inadvisable to entrust a large sum of money to a bank threatened with insolvency. For durable goods, the issue is the ongoing availability and quality of service and spare parts. For products that rely heavily on brand image, the threat of insolvency can have a negative affect on the brand's perception, which only compounds the problem.

These and other motives open the door for strong companies to lure away customers from their struggling competitors. A company could remain passive and wait for customers to come over on their own. Or it can seize the initiative and actively approach customers of struggling competitors with a variety of means. While this is a part of normal business practices in good times and bad times anyway, the difference is that the chances of success in a time of crisis grow, especially when the gap between the stronger and weaker competitors is widening.

In the U.S. banking market, many regional and community banks have actually benefited from the huge writeoffs and the resulting bad press of the big national banks. They have been acquiring a significant inflow of customer assets and have already started to use these funds to increase their market share on the lending and commercial financing side. On a similar note, many U.S. credit unions, with their stable, customer ("member") friendly image, have been attracting new assets, especially from customers who withdrew their funds from asset managers and investment fund providers who suffered from the market turmoil. In other countries, similar developments can be observed. In Germany, communal savings banks and cooperative banks report strong growth in assets. Consumers are shifting their funds from the large banks that they perceive as less safe to the smaller banks that are seen as safer.

Quick Solution 8: Develop New Business Models

Some insurance companies have introduced "price guarantee products" that run for one or more years. The move has resonated well with customers, who pay a relatively small upcharge. A desirable side effect is an increase in customer loyalty. Car manufacturers often offer large rebates, as we discussed earlier. In times of weak demand, these can amount to several thousand dollars. But in the spring and summer of 2008, gas prices became a top concern for most Americans, and traditional incentives were not working as well for certain companies. This prompted the automakers Suzuki and Chrysler to run promotions with gasoline as the incentive. Suzuki's "Free Gas for Summer" program offered free gas for three months on all new 2007 and 2008 models purchased between May 1 and June 30. They restricted the offer to customers who also signed 0% financing deals, with the overall intent to minimize the near-term financial impact of a new car. The most publicized promotion, however, was Chrysler's "Let's Refuel America" campaign. A customer had the choice of a traditional incentive, such as 0% financing or cash back, or a card that capped the price of gas at $2.99 for the first 12,000 miles per year, for three years.

Given the gas price plunge in late 2008, Suzuki's promotion ended up being a much better deal for consumers than Chrysler's. But consumers expected gas prices to rise, so Chrysler's promotion proved successful. Website traffic increased by 25% and showroom traffic by 35% after the campaign was launched.[9] Although only 5–10% of buyers ultimately chose the gas card over other incentives, this result met Chrysler's expectations. The automaker had not designed the offer as an attractive alternative for most car buyers. It designed "Let's Refuel America" to raise awareness of new Chrysler, Dodge, and Jeep models, and to get people into the showroom. This increase in "consideration" of Chrysler vehicles was enough for them to extend the program, ultimately through the end of July 2008.

Every crisis prompts customers to re-evaluate both their needs and their worries. Creative companies capitalize on these changes. In 2008, newly founded Kofler Energies introduced the following business model: it assumes the whole investment costs associated with energy-savings initiatives and guarantees the customer ongoing energy savings of 10%. Kofler retains all savings beyond the guaranteed 10%. This model addresses a problem – high upfront investment costs combined with limited access to credit – that becomes more common in times of crisis, and therefore has a clear appeal. The risk factor for Kofler Energies is to ensure that it has correctly calculated its ability to deliver on the guarantee and to exceed those promised levels in order to make money. The model would not make sense if Kofler were unsure whether it can regularly exceed the savings threshold of 10%. Vaillant, a maker of heating equipment, uses a similar model in California. Customers can pay off the upfront cost of their new heating installation through the energy savings they achieve. How much Vaillant earns depends on the customer's actual energy consumption.[10]

Another new business model is becoming common in information technology. Known as cloud computing, or SaaS (Software as a Service), a software company makes its products available over the Internet and guarantees a defined level of access. The customers reap an immediate benefit because they no longer need certain kinds of hardware, onsite installations, and long and costly implementation projects. Cloud computing implies a very different pricing model.

Traditionally, the software firm had a pricing structure composed of several components such as an upfront license payment, annual maintenance fees, and in some cases charges for implementation and/or hardware. Cloud computing lends itself to a monthly fee per user. The model becomes especially attractive in a time of crisis, because the high upfront costs are avoided. The customer can also better predict ongoing costs, which reduces the perceived risk. According to one estimate, the market for cloud computing is expected to triple to $42 billion annually by 2012 – despite the crisis.[11]

How quickly a company can develop and implement a new pricing model is a case-by-case question. Radically new business models are similar to long-term innovations, they take time to implement and require upfront investments. But many new business models allow for fast implementation, which can lead to quick increases in cash flow. New business models can thus offer ways to beat the crisis.

Summary

Customer behavior changes in times of crisis. As customers become more skittish about making purchases, aspects such as perceived risk and "hard" tangible advantages become more important, while image and other "nice to have" attributes move into the background. Financing and security issues count more than in good times. Companies can find ways to capitalize on these changes immediately. The following takeaways should be kept in mind:

- Companies have successfully overcome customer resistance by relieving customers of some of the transaction risks. Mechanisms include guarantees and warranties, success- or performance-based fees, or trial periods for machines.
- Companies need to adjust their communication strategy to match changes in customer buying criteria. Examples are price-oriented communication or value-based communication centered around clear cost-benefit advantages.
- Companies with strong balance sheets can use their financial power to their advantage in markets where private or corporate customers have sharply reduced access to credit. But companies need to have a good understanding of the increased risks before pursuing this strategy.
- During the crisis strong companies have better opportunities to lure customers away from vulnerable competitors.

- Companies should recognize changing or emerging customer needs and develop and implement new business models to meet them.

Changes in customer behavior can quickly become a danger to suppliers who are slow to respond. Conversely, companies that recognize these shifts and react quickly and decisively can turn a crisis into an opportunity. Markets are redistributed in times of crisis, not during good times.

Endnotes

1 "Moselferienpark denkt über Renditegarantie nach," *Eifelzeitung*, February 27, 2009, p. 20.
2 "Small Firms Resort to Freebies and Special Deals," WSJ.com, February 5, 2009.
3 "Small Firms Resort to Freebies and Special Deals," WSJ.com, February 5, 2009.
4 "Certainty in Uncertain Times," Hyundai Assurance, 2009.
5 For confidentiality reasons the name of this company is disguised.
6 Enercon owns more than 40% of the worldwide patents in the wind energy business.
7 "Messe Frankfurt unterstützt finanzschwache Anbieter," *Frankfurter Allgemeine Zeitung*, February 11, p. 15.
8 "Windradbauer überraschen mit ehrgeizigen Prognosen," *Financial Times Deutschland*, February 13, 2009, p. 14.
9 "Jim Press Sees Bright Future for Reborn Chrysler," corpmagazine.com, July 1, 2008.
10 "Small Firms Resort to Freebies and Special Deals," WSJ.com, February 5, 2009.
11 "Sparzwang beflügelt Wolkenkonzept," *Handelsblatt*, March 2, 2009, p. A2.

Chapter 5

Quick Solutions for Sales and the Salesforce

During a sales and revenue crisis, selling becomes the limiting factor to a company's further growth – or even its survival. Justus von Liebig's "law of the minimum" states that plant growth is controlled by the scarcest resource. Only by increasing the amount of the limiting nutrient can the plant thrive.[1] This principle was later applied to management theory.[2] According to this concept, managers should focus on the limiting factor, which in the current crisis is sales, in order to widen the "bottleneck." To improve sales performance, both efficiency (the relation between input and output) and effectiveness (output) must be taken into consideration.

Quick Solution 9: Boost Your Company's Sales Performance

The correlation between spending on selling activities and sales volume generally follows the sales-volume curve shown in Fig. 5.1. As the sales effort increases, the sales volume climbs at a decreasing rate. Curve A shows the situation before the crisis. The sales input and output each have an index of 100. The crisis moves the sales-volume curve to the right (curve B). With existing sales efforts of 100, sales volume drops to 75 on curve B. To maintain the sales volume at the former level of 100, it would be necessary to raise the sales effort to 125. The sales efficiency, or the ratio of output to input, drops by 25%, to 0.75 from 1. These numbers, which are realistic for the current crisis, demonstrate the seriousness of the situation.

What can be done in this situation? The answer depends on the shape and the shift of the sales-volume curve. In some cases it makes sense to simply spend more on selling activities. It is crucial to closely

H. Simon, *Beat the Crisis: 33 Quick Solutions for Your Company*, DOI 10.1007/978-1-4419-0823-0_5, © Hermann Simon 2010

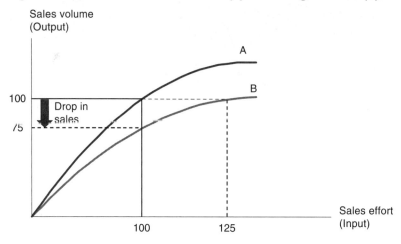

Fig. 5.1: The sales-volume curve before (A) and during the crisis (B)

examine individual selling activities, and to cut back on those activities that are inefficient. This can mean pursuing two goals at once: increasing sales efficiency and selectively cutting selling costs. During this crisis it will usually be impossible to defend previous sales levels, or it may not make financial sense to do so. In the case of Fig. 5.1, maintaining the former volume level would require a 25% increase in sales spending, an unrealistically high burden in view of limited financial resources. A more realistic scenario would be to mitigate the sales drop by aiming for a sales level of 85 or 90. If this is achieved and accompanied by selective cuts in sales and other costs, the situation looks much healthier than if sales volume falls to 75 while sales spending remains at 100. In accordance with the bottleneck concept, sales efforts should primarily focus on defending the sales level to the largest degree reasonable, not on cutting sales costs. Making sales cutbacks during a crisis is inadvisable and likely to further worsen the situation. This does not rule out selective savings, however. These can be considered if there will be no immediate impact on sales, such as for certain customer events, goodwill visits, or activities aimed at long-term image-boosting.

Improving sales performance becomes even more important in the case of significant cost remanence, that is, when costs can be reduced by only a small amount in the short term. This is the situation at T&L, a midsized screw manufacturer. Cost-cutting potential is low because the company's manufacturing processes are highly automated and its well-trained employees are already highly efficient. T&L has therefore turned its attention to sales. "Right now we're activating our contacts in all sectors," reports head of sales Torge Froehlich. "That means getting out there, presenting our products, and making offers." By stepping up its sales efforts, T&L aims to gain new customers in order to minimize the drop in revenues and prevent having to lay off highly skilled workers.

Speed is of the essence when it comes to sales solutions. They must be quickly implemented and have a rapid impact on sales. This is almost always the case for price-related solutions, but it requires a differentiated view in connection with the salesforce. It takes a long time to grow a salesforce by hiring new people. First, the right salespeople must be found and trained, and then they have to build a relationship of trust with each customer. This requires repeated visits and, thus, time. Salesforce enlargement by hiring and training people from the outside is therefore typically not suitable as a quick solution. A faster alternative is to lure experienced sellers with a network of contacts away from the competition. Typically, however, the rapid improvement in sales performance necessary in the crisis must result from a more efficient use of existing resources. Most of the quick solutions described below should, of course, also be pursued in more prosperous times. But if the limiting factor is manufacturing and not sales, managers pay more attention to these bottlenecks and neglect sales optimization.

Quick Solution 10: Increase Your Core Selling Time

One of the notorious problems in sales is that salespeople spend only a small portion of their time on actual sales-related activities. According to some sales experts, this portion can be as little as 15%.[3] Of course, this percentage depends on how "core" sales activities are defined. Figure 5.2 shows findings from a project in the metal industry in which "core selling time" comprises correspondence, customer visits, and other direct customer contacts. In this case, the salespeople spent less than half of their time (48%) on these activities.

Time spent traveling is also included in this 48%, so the sales employees' productive time is actually even less. Increasing the core selling time is a matter of process organization. How can sales forces be relieved of administration processes that do not have a direct sales impact? During a crisis there are plenty of underutilized in-house staff who can take over tasks such as making appointments, dealing with

Fig. 5.2: Breakdown of salespeople's activities

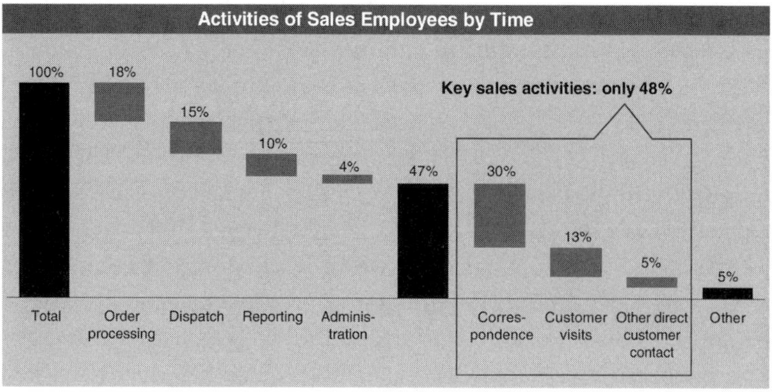

Activities of Sales Employees by Time

Key sales activities: only 48%

Total 100% | Order processing 18% | Dispatch 15% | Reporting 10% | Administration 4% | 47% | Correspondence 30% | Customer visits 13% | Other direct customer contact 5% | Other 5%

inquiries, and following up customer requests. Reshuffles of this kind are easy to implement and lead to a direct increase in the time spent on key sales activities.

Another effective tool to improve sales efficiency is professional visit and route planning in order to minimize unproductive travel time. However, the introduction of such a system usually takes substantial time, because the necessary data have to be collected and analyzed. A simple and extremely effective quick solution for sales managers is to relieve them of driving. Sales managers and salespersons often clock up 40,000 or more miles on the road annually. Assuming an average speed of 40 mph, this equates to 1,000 h of unproductive time behind the wheel each year. During a crisis, why not have some of the under-utilized employees serve as drivers? For the salespeople this means increased productivity, because they can use the time to prepare in more depth, to compile offers, or simply to relax. Incidentally, this option is recommended for many managers even in a non-crisis situation. Being driven is the simplest way of buying time, and in the crisis it can enhance the sales performance at no extra cost, because the drivers are idle anyway.

Quick Solution 11: Visit Customers More Selectively

When optimizing customer visit planning, it is important to consider which customers should be visited and how often.[4] In most of our projects we find that sales people tend to treat all customers the same in this respect. But paying the same number of calls to every client results in considerable sales inefficiency, because customers typically have very different "values." Why should a C-customer receive just as many visits as an A-customer?

The following case of a component manufacturer illustrates how widely customer values can differ. As shown in Figure 5.3, 10% of this company's customers generate 74.4% of the revenue. Even more importantly, however, the "bottom" 50% of customers (numbering over 1,000) account for a mere 2.2% of revenue. In other words, salespeople who spend equal amounts of time on each customer have failed in their visit and route planning, and are extremely inefficient. Such mistakes can be rectified within a few weeks by introducing a selective visit planning system. These systems can give sales performance a significant boost with no additional costs.

Another frequent problem is that salespeople tend to visit their preferred customers more frequently. In a project in the U.S. medical technology market the salespeople spent almost all their time with accounts where they were highly welcome, but they had little to gain since their products were used almost exclusively anyway. These customers are "buddies" and a lot of time is devoted to chatting, wining, and dining with little to no impact on sales. In this case, it would have been much more effective visiting accounts where the company had a low share. But that would also have been much less convenient for the salesperson because the reception is often rather hostile. This is why many sales reps avoid visiting these accounts, although they may have a high sales potential.

Fig. 5.3: Revenue distribution of a component manufacturer by customer

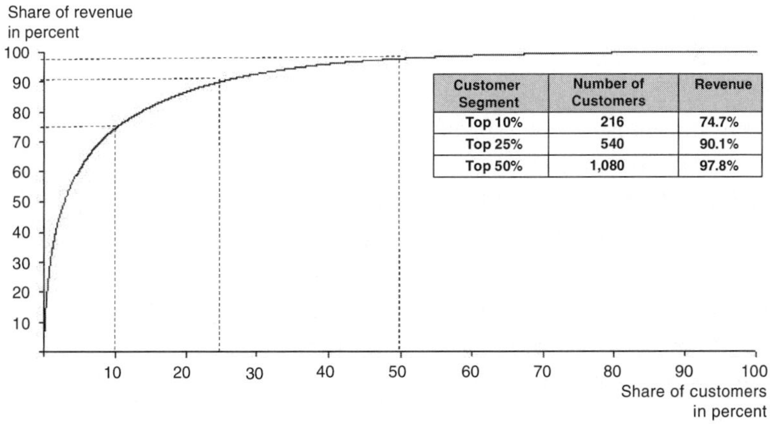

Customer Segment	Number of Customers	Revenue
Top 10%	216	74.7%
Top 25%	540	90.1%
Top 50%	1,080	97.8%

Quick Solution 12: Strengthen Direct Sales

Direct sellers have natural advantages in times of crisis: they have direct access to their customers and do not depend on intermediaries such as wholesalers or retailers. In the customer contact situation they usually have the sole attention of the customer. In this sense, they don't have to fight for share of attention or share of shelf. At the other end of the scale are companies that do not conduct their own sales activities. Condemned to a passive role, they are helpless if the order flow dries up in the crisis. Examples include Chinese manufacturers of consumer goods, toys, and similar products that receive all of their orders via the Chinese website alibaba.com.[5] In the current crisis thousands of these companies vanished because people stopped placing orders this way. They had no direct access to their customers.

One direct seller that is doing well despite the crisis is Home & House. They sell blinds, awnings, windows, and canopies through a network of 600 direct sales representatives. Since its target segment (private family homes) is clearly defined, customers can be targeted very specifically. In spite of the crisis and a tough winter, Home & House expects this year's revenue to match year-ago levels. This is a very ambitious goal, and direct selling is the key factor.

Another direct seller that is coping well with the crisis is Tupperware, the manufacturer of plastic containers and other kitchen items. The distribution model is based on "Tupperware Consultants," a salesforce more than 2.2 million strong working on a commission basis. The company is essentially selling products that are expensive and that nobody really needs. One would expect this sector to be hit hard by the crisis. However, Tupperware managed to boost sales by 8% in 2008 and even had a strong fourth quarter when the economic crisis was in full swing. Direct selling was a key factor for this success.

Also TV pitchmen are doing well in the crisis: "During recessions people not only tend to stay home and watch a lot of television, but also become more susceptible to the type of DIY products often featured in infomercials and more in need of the pick-me-up thrill of snagging a perceived bargain. 'Call in now and I'll throw in an extra set for free.' "[6]

If a company already conducts direct sales, it now makes good sense to step up these activities. One way of doing this is to involve in-house staff as described in Quick Solution 15. In some cases it may also be possible to move away from distributors and to start canvasing customers directly. Setting up a professional direct sales operation, on the other hand, is a long-term option with a more strategic character. However, exploiting the immediate opportunities of direct sales in the short term can help to soften the blow of declining sales.

The solutions relating to direct sales can also be applied to direct marketing. In Chapter 7, we will see an example of an oil tank manufacturer that decided to directly distribute brochures to households. The brochures contained information about the company's inspection, cleaning, and maintenance services for oil tanks. Any kind of direct access to the customer has potential value in the crisis and should be looked at closely.

Quick Solution 13: Penetrate New Customer Segments

Where and how can falling sales be offset, at least partially? The most obvious option is to better exploit the customer base in the company's target segment. A similar approach is to increase the share of wallet among existing customers. It is enlightening to examine this option from a market share perspective. If a company holds 10% of a particular market, 90% of the market remains unutilized. The unserved share of the market is nine times larger than the served share. Even if sales decline by 25%, the unexploited market potential is still 67.5% of the original potential, or 6.8 times higher than the original sales level. Even a supplier with a 30% share of wallet has 70% of the demand covered by competitors.

These remarks come with a proviso. Although the described potentials exist, exploiting them is much harder during a crisis than when times are good. What's more, increasing the market or supply share is more likely to trigger aggressive responses from competitors, and ultimately a price war. Companies must therefore proceed with great care when pushing further into existing market and customer segments.

The prospects are different when it comes to penetrating new customer segments. These segments can cover previously unserved regions, target industries or price ranges. Entering a new segment is usually a lengthy, costly process; in this case it is of only limited value as a quick solution for tackling the crisis. However, this does not necessarily apply if the new segment is close to an existing one, either geographically or in product terms. In such cases, it might be possible to tap the segment quickly and without a large upfront investment.

A construction company from a rural area, for example, was facing a drop in demand from local customers. In response, it decided to enlarge its operating radius from 75 to 150 miles, thereby including two cities, each with a population of one million. It submitted tenders for small projects that could be conducted without extra capacity, and landed several contracts straightaway. Although the company probably won't make much money with these projects, it can keep its qualified workforce. It plans to return to its original operating radius when orders pick up again. For many companies, limited regional expansion opens up sales potential that can be harnessed quickly. An opportunistic entrant does not have to be as wary of oligopolistic reactions in a new region, and can be more aggressive in pricing. There is a danger that the local incumbents will retaliate by pushing into the entrant's home market, but this is unlikely if this local market is small (such as in the case above). A quick push into technologically similar market segments or adjacent price categories can also open up new opportunities. However, it is vital to remember that customers' reluctance to buy during a crisis, and the competitors' fiercer defense of "their" segments, can make it more difficult to increase sales in this way.

Another example is offered by a manufacturer of power tools. Its premium-quality products used to be sold exclusively to professional skilled workers. In response to the crisis, the company decided to sell a particular product category through do-it-yourself-stores as well. Within a few weeks this category accounted for 5% of the company's revenue.[7]

Quick Solution 14: Offer Special Incentives

Incentive systems are important tools for motivating salespeople. Most incentive systems are revenue-based, but forms based on other parameters, such as margins or price realization, have gained ground in recent years. Ongoing incentive programs are usually accompanied by one-time incentives that vary widely and change over time.

The right incentives have a quick impact, which makes them suitable for tackling the crisis. In one project we recommended an anti-discount incentive for the salesforce: the larger the discount granted, the lower the salesperson's commission percentage. Within two months the average discount had fallen to 14% from 16%, with no customer or volume losses. This equates to a price increase of 200 basis points.[8] These 200 basis points led to a 50% margin increase, to 6% from 4%. Incentive systems should be designed with great care, as they may lead to unanticipated and unwarranted results. Calls for sales- and revenue-boosting incentives naturally become louder during a crisis. But it is also crucial to bear in mind that such incentives often work at the expense of margins and profits. And a company's chance of survival does not increase if it sells more units but its margins continue to shrink.

Quick Solution 15: Redeploy In-House Staff to Sales

As sales drop during the crisis, overcapacity in manufacturing and other in-house functions will emerge. Conversely, this can be expressed as undercapacity in sales and marketing. The logical response is to increase capacity in these areas, preferably without incurring higher costs. This can be done by transferring resources from non-sales-related activities to marketing (for example, from training to advertising) or other activities that quickly promote sales. Most important, however, is to consider transferring non-sales employees, who are underutilized and who cost money, into sales. This approach kills two birds with one stone. First, it prevents office idling and improves morale. Second, it can boost sales, even if the successes are modest. It is generally known that office staff are not ideal sellers, otherwise they would have gone into sales from the start. This may be true in many cases, but certainly not in all. The main barriers here are related to culture and leadership. The case of Wuerth, the global market leader for assembly products, proves that these barriers can be overcome. Wuerth, a $12 billion company, has a pronounced sales culture. It employs 65,000 people, half of them are in sales. During a crisis in the 1990s, Wuerth redeployed almost 10% of its office staff into the sales force within a year. According to one study, successful companies rotate staff to other functions around five times more often than less successful companies.[9] We advised a manufacturer of premium leisure products to organize a series of sales shows using internal staff in the Middle East and Asia; these regions are still seeing growth despite the crisis. The outcome was successful here, too.

A well-known manufacturer of designer furniture was guarded about sending in-house employees out to meet its discerning customers, so these employees were deployed to telephone selling instead. "Although they sell less than the professionals, they still do make sales," reports the CEO. "And some of them find that they have a real knack for it." This is an added bonus, because good salespeople are few and far between. If a company's office staff are underutilized, it is always better to involve them in sales than to leave them in the office doing nothing.

The first stage in adopting this kind of quick solution is to identify in-house employees who would be suitable for selling activities. It is crucial that they are willing to be reassigned; otherwise the solution is doomed to failure. Next, training in sales techniques must be provided, although this need not consume too many resources because the new sellers are already familiar with the products. If the workers and the trade unions have no objections, this solution can be implemented within a few weeks. It has a quick impact and does not generate significant added costs.

Quick Solution 16: Lure Salespeople Away from Competitors

As an alternative to enlarging the salesforce by reassigning in-house employees, the crisis opens opportunities to lure salespeople away from competitors. For strong companies this is a practical and appealing option. One should keep in mind, however, that employing new people costs money, unless they are being hired to replace weaker sellers from the existing team.

In normal circumstances it is difficult and expensive to draw good salespeople away from the competition. This changes during a crisis, especially if a competitor is struggling. In this case, good salespeople become more willing to switch employers. What's more, they might be prepared to sacrifice a pay rise, or even to accept a drop in their income. Unlike in-house staff, they are experienced sales professionals. And if they come from the same product and market segment, they usually do not need costly, time-consuming training. They can be deployed at short notice, have an existing network of customer contacts, and can achieve rapid sales and revenue success. Such solutions are, however, suitable only for companies whose market position or financial power make them less susceptible to the crisis than their weakened competitors. During the crisis, strong companies will become even stronger on the sales front.

Quick Solution 17: Mobilize Top Sales Excellence

Like almost everything in life, sales performance can be depicted with a Gaussian curve (normal distribution). Most companies are aware of this distribution in relation to revenue, but much less so with regard to profit or contribution margin per sales employee. Neither are they very knowledgeable about the causes of this distribution. When asked "What is it that makes top sellers stand out from the rest?" most managers give replies such as:

> "It's all about personality."
> "They're just born sellers."
> "They put more effort into it than the others."

These reasons may be important, but they still do not answer the question of what top sales people do differently.

In the case of Retelo, a major automotive manufacturer (with revenues of over $6.5 billion),[10] these considerations were the starting point for an immediate program to boost sales performance. The aim of the Retelo project was to share the knowledge and success strategies of the top sellers as widely as possible with the entire sales team. First, the top sellers were identified by an internal data analysis of their contributions to sales, revenue, and profit. Initial discussions with executives and sales managers revealed that these sellers had a strong ego. In addition, they rarely interacted with other sales people or passed on their expertise. It was therefore not easy to tap into their know-how and make it accessible to the rest of the team.

Group and one-to-one discussions were then held with all of the top sellers to overcome their reluctance to share information. Some of these discussions lasted up to five hours. Unsurprisingly, the willingness to share information varied from person to person. It emerged that this knowledge sharing failed not because of deliberate resistance, but because the top sellers were often unaware of their own sales tactics and applied them intuitively. Six key traits of outstanding salespeople were identified as a result of the discussions. Without going into too much detail here, all six characteristics contribute to what can be termed as "value selling." It transpired, for instance, that the top sellers had studied the business processes and cost effectiveness of their customers in much greater depth than the normal sales people had. They were also more persuasive when describing product benefits, and able to quantify these benefits in more detail. In other words, they knew more about their customers' needs and how the company's products met them. Considerable differences were also identified in relation to sales tactics, argumentation techniques, and knowledge of competitors. Although some of the insights gained from the discussions concerned general selling tactics, most were vendor-, product-, and customer-specific. Boosting sales performance by enhancing the team's overall expertise therefore calls for an in-depth study of the individual business in question. It is not possible to change sellers' personalities, but it is possible to share with them the knowledge, argumentation, and methods of the top salespeople in order to improve results.

The findings from the analysis of the top sellers' tactics formed the foundation for a systematic program of workshops for the rest of the sales team, including case studies and practical exercises. The workshops were conducted without further delay. Six weeks passed between the project kickoff and the actual implementation. Sales performance improved within one month. As a result of the project, Retelo expects a revenue boost of about 150 basis points, or in absolute terms $98 million. If this goal is achieved, the improved sales performance will contribute to securing some 400 jobs at Retelo.

Quick Solution 18: Step Up Cross-Selling

Every company has an existing customer base. The problem is that many of these customers buy only one product from the range, or perhaps just a few. Bank customers, for example, buy an average of 2.6 products from their bank.[11] Similarly, a restaurant-goer might order a main dish, but not a starter or a dessert. The tactic of cross-selling aims to motivate existing customers to buy as many products as possible from the supplier's range, instead of only one or two. It therefore has an aim similar to bundling, which we will examine in the next chapter. However, cross-selling is primarily a sales tactic (the sales person is incentivized to sell several products) whereas bundling is a price tactic (the buyer pays less for the bundle than for the sum of the items it contains). Taken together, these two approaches can reinforce each other.

Effective cross-selling increases revenue and boosts customer loyalty, making it a suitable tool for countering the drop in sales caused by the crisis. The analysis of bank customers' product usage[12]

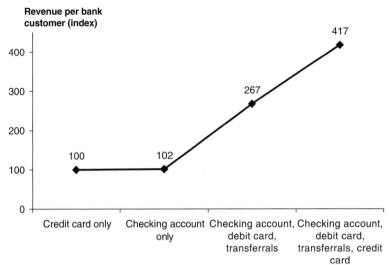

Fig. 5.4: Revenue per bank customer by products used

Revenue per bank customer (index)

Source: Simon-Kucher & Partners

supports this tenet. Figure 5.4 shows that customers who have a checking account and a debit card, and who make transferrals from this account, generate about 2.6 times more revenue than customers who have a checking account or a credit card only. If a credit card is added to the mix, the revenue climbs to more than four times that of single-product customers. In addition, customers who use several products are more loyal to the bank. These customers are therefore particularly important for the bank's success, especially during a crisis, when less loyal customers tend to jump ship.

One advantage of cross-selling is that it can be quickly implemented. In practice, however, organizational or behavior-related challenges often need to be overcome. These can have various causes, the main one being the sellers' lack of product knowledge. People who are used to selling bank products do not need to know much about selling insurance. This is why the all-finance approach of cross-selling bank and insurance products has failed to take off so far. Inconsistent incentivization can also make cross-selling more difficult. A large manufacturer of medical technology allocated its product and service businesses in separate divisions. Without an explicit cross-selling incentive, the product sellers had no motivation to sell service contracts as well (and vice versa). Last but not least, salespeople tend to focus on selling their primary product during the customer encounter. This is already a challenging task, so they are naturally reluctant to draw the customer's attention away from the primary product.

A simple and effective way to improve cross-selling is to use checklists related to customer needs. Sellers at Visio Lumina, a large photo and video retailer,[13] go through a checklist of accessories (camera bags, batteries, storage media, tripods, microphones, filters, and so on) with every customer who buys a camera or a camcorder. Sales of these "secondary" products have climbed by 30% as a result of this tactic. A number of banks are successfully using similar checklists to step up their cross-selling activities. One bank specializing in home loans recently introduced a structured questionnaire that its advisors use to systematically determine customers' financial status and needs. This enables the advisors to create tailor-made financial packages for each customer and increase the cross-selling rate.

Every reasonable opportunity to cross-sell should be grasped during the crisis. This calls for careful preparation. Given the importance of rapid implementation and impact, high-affinity products are the most suitable for cross-selling.

Quick Solution 19: Expand Your Sales Portfolio

Falling sales and a loss of customers lead to a drop in sales efficiency, and sometimes even to an underutilized salesforce. One possible solution is to expand the range of products sold by adding items from other suppliers. The new products should ideally be complementary to the existing portfolio, not in direct competition with it. Additionally, they should require similar sales competencies; otherwise the same difficulties sometimes associated with cross-selling (described above) could emerge. If the new products are too different from the existing ones, the sales team may need extra training. This takes time, however, and does not meet the need for quick implementation and quick impact. It is also helpful if customers have trust in the salesperson's knowledge of the expanded product range.

Many cooperative sales ventures work both ways: each partner adds products of the other to its own sales portfolio. This has two advantages. First, each salesforce is utilized more effectively and earns commissions. Second, the sales volume of a given product increases because both companies are selling it at the same time.

In the case of two complementary manufacturers of building materials, each salesforce started selling certain products from the other's portfolio. Not only did both companies increase their revenues, they also avoided salesforce cutbacks and mass layoffs in production. In another example, two food manufacturers with strong but under-utilized salesforces took the same approach. Today, their sales capacity is used more effectively and the threat of a revenue slump has eased. This is a "win–win" situation for both companies.

Similar action has been taken in the insurance, investment and home loan sectors, and the pharmaceutical industry. Aiming to increase sales instead of making cutbacks works in many cases. A large insurance company, which outsourced 92% of its sales team to a direct sales organization, is a case in point. In the subsequent months, the insurance posted a strong revenue increase and strengthened its market position. The CEO brushes aside concerns of becoming too dependent on the sales partner. "The model works," he reports. "Despite what the skeptics said, there's no sting in the tail."[14]

Summary

A sales crisis means that sales form the limiting factor for a company's further development or survival. The company must therefore do all it can to maximize its sales efficiency and effectiveness. The key takeaways of this chapter are as follows:

- Sales efficiency drops sharply during a crisis. Companies should counter this by enhancing their sales efforts.
- The seriousness of the current crisis makes it unlikely that the solutions suggested will completely counteract falling sales. The slump can, however, be partially offset.
- Activities should focus on defending or stabilizing the sales level, not on cutting sales costs.
- If cost remanence is strong, boosting the sales performance becomes even more important because it is the only way of avoiding a profit and liquidity disaster.
- Speed of implementation and impact should be a top priority for sales-related solutions in the crisis.
- Increasing the time spent on core selling activities is even more important during the crisis than at other times. As more internal resources are available, this improvement should be easier to achieve.
- New customer acquisitions should focus on neighboring segments that can be served opportunistically.

- Redeploying in-house staff to the salesforce is a cost-neutral solution that boosts sales and can improve morale.
- In the crisis, companies with strong sales and financial power can lure salespeople away from struggling competitors.
- Top sellers have skills that can be shared with the entire sales team.
- By adding another supplier's products into its sales portfolio, a company can make better use of capacity and increase sales at the same time. Ideally, the products of both companies are swapped.

It is surprising how many sales options are available for stabilizing revenue and profit. The key is to pursue them with determination, but after thoughtful consideration. The quick sales solutions must be analyzed thoroughly and chosen with care.

Endnotes

1 See William H. Brock, *Justus von Liebig: The Chemical Gatekeeper*, Cambridge: Cambridge University Press 1995 and Ernst F. Schwenk, *Sternstunden der frühen Chemie*, Munich: C.H. Beck 1998.

2 See Wolfgang Mewes, *Mit Nischenstrategie zur Marktführerschaft*, Zurich: Orell Füssli 2000, and Kerstin Friedrich, *Erfolgreich durch Spezialisierung*, Heidelberg: Redline 2007.

3 This percentage was mentioned to the author in a discussion with the late sales guru Heinz Goldmann, who died in 2005.

4 "Was 2009 auf den Vertrieb zukommt," salesBUSINESS, December 2008.

5 Production and other B2B services are offered via alibaba.com, especially by Chinese companies.

6 "Secrets of the TV Pitchmen," *Fortune*, April 20, 2009, pp. 64–70.

7 Personal communication between Philip Grothe, a partner at Simon-Kucher & Partners, and the managing director of the power tool manufacturer.

8 A basis point is one hundredth of a percentage point, so 200 basis points correspond to two (absolute) percentage points.

9 See Hermann Simon, *Hidden Champions of the 21st Century*, New York: Springer 2009, Chap. 9.

10 Name disguised for confidentiality reasons.

11 See Georg Wübker, *Power Pricing für Banken*, second edition, Frankfurt: Campus 2008.

12 See Jan Engelke, Georg Wübker, Maren Jäger, "Loyalität muss sich lohnen," *die bank*, October 2007, pp. 58–63.

13 Name disguised for confidentiality reasons.

14 "Aachen-Münchener Versicherung knackt die Fünf-Milliarden-Marke," *Frankfurter Allgemeine Zeitung*, February 6, 2009, p. 15.

Chapter 6

Quick Solutions for Managing Offers and Prices

In Chapter 2, we dealt with the relation between supply and demand. During a crisis, supply outpaces demand, leading to unfavorable pricing and competitive outcomes. While it is hardly possible to overcome these negative effects altogether, it is crucial to mitigate their impact. What measures are effective against these threatening developments? Supply needs to be reduced as quickly as possible while fighting the price decreases. Price cuts may be unavoidable in the crisis, but they must be implemented intelligently. By proceeding cautiously it is possible to selectively increase prices in the crisis.

Quick Solution 20: Cut Your Volume

As discussed in Chapter 2, a volume reduction usually harms profit less than a price reduction. In our illustrative example, a price cut of 5% led to a profit decline of 50%, whereas a volume reduction of 5% only caused a profit decline of 20%. Therefore, limitation of supply is one of the first and foremost steps to combating the crisis. The goals are different from those described in Chapter 3, where we discussed capacity and volume reductions (through layoffs, reduced working hours or the closure of plants) aimed at lowering costs. From a market perspective, the primary goals of volume reductions are price stabilization and reduction of competitive pressures. However, both goals of volume restriction – cost reduction and price stabilization – have welcome effects on profit and cash flow.

The disastrous results of oversupply are illustrated by the automotive industry. Per 2009 the worldwide annual automotive manufacturing capacity is 90 million units. However, in 2008 only 55 million cars were sold, and for 2009 only 50 million units or less are expected to be sold.[1] This results in a global overcapacity of at least 50%. In the U.S., total

H. Simon, *Beat the Crisis: 33 Quick Solutions for Your Company*,
DOI 10.1007/978-1-4419-0823-0_6, © Hermann Simon 2010

industrial production capacity in use was less than 70%, resulting in about 50% overcapacity.[2] As long as such imbalances exist, pricing will remain volatile. Continued overcapacities and the physical presence of an overwhelming number of unsold cars will generate ever more radical price cuts in the attempt to find buyers. Burkhard Weller, CEO of car dealership Autoweller, corroborates this view, "The automotive crisis has nothing to do with the financial crisis. Quite simply, too many cars have been produced for years. Production must be reduced to give prices a chance to recover."[3] Similar developments can be observed for consumer electronics, hotel rooms, airlines, machinery, and many another products with excess supply.

A few years ago, the CEO of a large engineering company shared the following insight with the author, "It's impossible to be profitable in my industry. All suppliers have overcapacities. Whenever a new project comes on the market, one competitor is desperate for this project and quotes a suicidal price. In some cases we are this guy, in others it's a competitor. Although four suppliers who know each other well hold 80% of the world market, none of them makes a profit." My answer to this problem was evident, "As long as the overcapacities exist this situation is not going to change." The industry became profitable only after one of the four suppliers left the market and the others reduced their capacities. None of the companies would have been able to improve the situation singlehandedly. Cutting the overall supply was the key.

These considerations underline how critical volume control is to surviving the crisis. The laws of economics work mercilessly as long as the imbalance between supply and demand prevails. When a company or an industry dumps too much product into the marketplace, prices and margins inevitably decline. The problem starts in the plant. There are pressures to maintain the volumes that are necessary to keep workers busy, but, at the same time, exceeding demand inevitably affects prices and competition. The cost structure plays an important role in this context. A combination of low variable costs and high fixed costs may be a blessing in good times but become a curse during a crisis. High fixed costs call for distribution over large unit numbers. At the same time, low variable unit costs still yield a positive contribution margin despite low prices. These conditions exert pressure on the salesforce to accept lower prices in order to achieve the highest possible sales volume.

In a downturn, this volume pressure must be eased by management. Many companies in various industries have reacted by reducing working hours and closing down production sites. BASF, the world's largest chemical company, shut down 80 plants worldwide; while

Dow Chemical closed 20 plants and idled 180.[4] "Delta Airlines and American Airlines further reduce the number of flights. Delta will scale back its foreign capacity by 15% and its domestic capacity will be 75% smaller compared with a year earlier."[5] These are the right moves. But in view of the extent to which demand has dropped they are not always sufficient.

So far, we have mainly discussed individual companies. In these cases, the necessity of volume reduction is evident. But what should a company do if competitors refuse to come along and instead try to use the emerging demand/supply gaps to increase their market shares? This is a perfect analogy to pricing in an oligopoly. In an oligopoly, a price increase can be the optimal solution for a company. However, if a company's competitors sustain current prices or even lower prices, a price increase by that company is a very risky move. The same is true for volume reductions. If the competitors don't play along or even push more volume into the market the plan can easily backfire. A company would lose market share and even endanger its long-term market position.

It is therefore essential to keep a close eye on the competition and to exert all legally allowed influence to get the industry as a whole to reduce volume. Direct agreements with competitors regarding volume and price are prohibited by antitrust laws. But it is not illegal to signal one's own intentions with regard to volume reductions. A company that plans to reduce its volume can signal this intention to the market. Part of effective signaling is announcing that one's own market share will be defended, an implicit suggestion to competitors that they decrease their volumes as well. The potential for retaliation should also be signaled to prevent competitors from trying to take advantage of the volume reduction.

Consistency between announcement and actual conduct is essential to an effective signaling strategy. Once a volume reduction has been proclaimed it must be put into effect within the announced time frame. A company must also make sure that its sales organization observes the limitations. If management announces a volume reduction, but the salesforce continues to use aggressive prices to push larges quantities into the market, the competitors are going to strike back, harming the entire industry. All aspects of oligopolistic pricing apply equally to the management of volume reductions.[6]

In a crisis, chances are good that the competitors will understand the overall picture and behave in a sensible manner. In many sectors, industrywide reductions of capacities can indeed be observed. In addition to the capacity restrictions in industrial sectors such as automotive, steel or chemistry we see similar action in tourism, car rentals, and other service fields.[7]

Quick Solution 21: Cut Prices Intelligently

In a crisis, price management moves to the forefront. "One of the most important decisions in this recession is what to do about prices. In booms you don't have to get pricing exactly right. Now you do," says *Fortune* columnist Geoff Colvin.[8] An indispensable requirement for intelligent pricing is a precise understanding of the relationship between price and sales. This understanding is essential in a crisis because the price-sales curve and price thresholds are shifting.

The most frequent and counterproductive reactions to the crisis have been large and premature price cuts, often implemented in the form of high discounts. How can this counterproductive behavior be explained? In most cases it is an attempt to maintain the current level of sales and employment. To discuss this we look at Figure 6.1. Before the crisis the price-sales curve A was valid. One million units were sold at the price of $100. The resulting revenue is $100 million. With variable unit costs of $60 and fixed costs of $30 million, we get a profit of

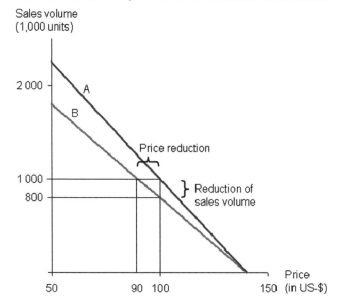

Fig. 6.1: Sales reduction or price cuts as a reaction to the crisis

$10 million. How does the crisis affect the price-sales curve? We assume that curve B in Figure 6.1 applies in the crisis. For any price the sales volume is 20% lower. If we leave the price at $100, sales fall to 800,000 units. The massive volume reduction induces a strong temptation to lower the price to $90 in order to maintain the sales volume at 1 million units. Employment would be guaranteed and layoffs avoided. In terms of profit, however, the two alternatives of keeping the price at $100 or cutting it to $90 are very different. If we keep the price at $100 and accept the 20% drop in volume we still get a profit of $2 million. With a reduced price of $90 and an unchanged sales volume of 1 million units, however, the profit falls to zero.

The insight that a volume reduction is preferable to a price reduction is necessary but not sufficient to make a decision. The next question addresses by how much the volume and/or the price should be lowered in order to get the highest achievable profit under the new circumstances. This question can be answered precisely and reliably only with the help of the price-sales curve. It is the reverse of "How much do I sell at a given price?" The CEO of a premium car manufacturer once asked the author, "How many units of my top model can the world live with if I want to maintain the current price level?" To determine the answer, volume and price must be considered simultaneously, requiring the quantification of the price-sales curve. Several modern methods are available and applicable even under the time pressure induced by the crisis. For instance, systematic expert judgment can be collected within a company in just a few days. The relevance of knowing the exact curve is illustrated by the two seemingly similar curves in Figure 6.2. The left curve shows the case from Figure 6.1. For any price the sales volume is

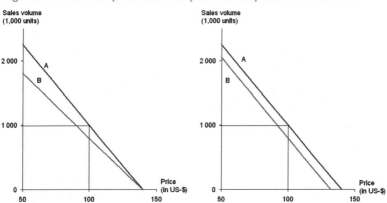

Fig. 6.2: Different implications despite similar price-sales curves

20% lower. On the right side the pre-crisis curve A is identical, but the crisis causes sales to go down by 200,000 units for any price, which means that curve B is a parallel to curve A.

For a price of $100 we get the same sales results in both cases. Due to the crisis the sales volumes fall to 800,000 units. To defend the former sales volume of 1 million units the price would have to be lowered to $90 in the left figure, but only to $92 in the right figure. The differences between the two cases seem minimal. However, this is not true for optimal prices and volumes. In the left case, one gets the maximum profit by leaving the price at the old level of $100 and accepting the full volume decline of 200,000 units or 20%. Compared to the initial situation the profit goes down to $2 million from $10 million. In the right case, the maximum profit is achieved when the price is lowered to $96 and the company accepts a decline in sales volume of 10% to 900,000 units.[9] The profit falls to $2.4 million. Although both curves look very similar at first sight there are massive differences in the optimal reactions to each, especially with regard to the sales volume. The reduction in sales in the left case is twice as high as in the case on the right. This simple example underlines how important it is to quantify the price-sales curve as precisely as possible. Ignorance or wrong assumptions in this matter can lead to serious mistakes in dealing with the crisis.

The following statements from two top managers in the automotive industry show how strongly views regarding price and volume in a downturn can diverge. In 2003, Richard Wagoner, CEO of General Motors from June 2000 to April 2009, said, "Fixed costs are extremely high in our industry. We realized that in a crisis we fare better with low prices than by reducing volume. After all, in contrast to some competitors, we still make money with this strategy."[10] Wendelin Wiedeking, the CEO of Porsche, has a very different opinion, "We have a policy of keeping prices stable to protect our brand and to prevent a drop in prices for used cars. When demand goes down we reduce production but don't lower our prices."[11] Wiedeking made this statement several years ago and confirmed it again in the crisis of 2009, "One thing is clear to us: We will not flood the markets with cars for which there is no demand. We always produce one car less than the market demands."[12]

General Motors and Porsche cannot be compared one-to-one with regard to market position, cost situation, and manufacturing flexibility. However, it requires no further explanation to determine which company fared better. Porsche has been the world's most profitable automotive manufacturer in terms of profit margin for several years. General Motors has been a money loser for years and became insolvent in 2009. The polar positions of Wagoner and Wiedeking point to the core of the problem. A crisis inevitably means that sales volume drops if the price is kept at the current level. It does not mean, however, that sales remain at the current level if the price is cut. There are two reasons for this result. First, the price-sales curve goes down in a crisis: at a given price, customers buy fewer units. Second, price cuts don't result in the desired sales increase because the competitors usually follow suit with their own price cuts, that is, the relative prices hardly change. Hopes for a higher market share and an unchanged sales volume dissolve into thin air. In a crisis – as already outlined in Chapter 1 – customers don't refuse to buy because prices are too high, but because they are insecure and save their money for an uncertain future. Price cuts within realistic ranges do little to alleviate this feeling of insecurity. To overcome this resistance price cuts must be unusually high. Such extreme price cuts, however, ruin margins and, even more dangerous, can ignite price wars that will further destroy margins for a long time to come. Conversely, hoping to get away in a crisis without making any price concessions at all is also unrealistic.

If price reductions are unavoidable they should be made in a way that minimizes negative effects and maximizes the positive impact on sales and profit. It must be understood that the interest of the seller is fundamentally different for price cuts and for price increases. With a price increase, the seller prefers that the customer does not notice the increase, thereby preventing sales volume from decreasing. With a price cut, the seller prefers that the customer notices the decline in price so that sales volume increases. Thus, in the case of a price cut the supplier should strive to increase price elasticity by clearly communicating the lower price to customers.

Empirical studies show that the positive effects on sales of a price reduction are considerably higher when the price cut is communicated through advertising, double placements in stores, special displays, and so on. While the positive effects on sales are highly welcome in the crisis, communication budgets have typically been cut. This presents a dilemma: on the one hand, price reductions have increased, on the other hand, there is less money to communicate these reductions.[13]

Apart from the general question concerning whether prices should be lowered at all, special attention must be paid to the extent of price cuts in the crisis. The shape of the price-sales curve determines the optimal extent of a price reduction. The linear price-sales curves shown in Figure 6.2 are good approximations for price changes that stay close to the original price. For more drastic price cuts or price increases, however, we have to assume the existence of price thresholds.[14] Figure 6.3 shows the price-sales curve with price thresholds.

In the pre-crisis curve A the upper price threshold is $110 and the lower price threshold is $90. When the price moves beyond these thresholds, the sales effect of a price change increases drastically compared to the effect of price changes within the interval between $90 and $110. Beyond this interval price elasticity is markedly higher on both sides. How does the crisis affect the price thresholds? We already know that the price-sales curve shifts downward, that is, for any price sales are lower. In addition, we have to assume that the price thresholds go down. In our example with curve B the upper price threshold drops to $105 and the lower one drops to $85.

This new situation has drastic consequences for pricing in the crisis. The new optimal price can only be determined if the price-sales curves and especially the price thresholds are precisely known. In the case without price thresholds in Figure 6.1 we have seen that maintaining the original price is the optimal solution. The profit falls from $10 to $2 million, the highest possible profit in this situation. What is the optimal price with the price thresholds in Figure 6.3? If we reduce the price within the flat part of the curve the sales volume increases only slightly and profit drops sharply. For example, if the price is reduced to $90, profit drops to zero. Sales volume increases noticeably only when the price drops below the lower price threshold. It is only then that the increased sales volume can overcompensate for the loss in unit margin. However, this only happens if the left branch of the curve is very steep.

Such a situation is illustrated in Figure 6.3. Here the optimal price in the crisis drops to $78. 1.8 million units more are sold. With a value of −5.7, price elasticity is very high.[15] Profit is $2.4 million. While this is a lot lower than the $10 million in the original situation before the crisis, it is higher than the profit of $2 million, which results if the original price of $100 is maintained.

This calculation illustrates that great caution is necessary when cutting prices in a crisis. In this example a price reduction to $85 would aggravate the profit situation. Only when the price drops clearly below the threshold of $85 does sales volume increase sufficiently to offset the margin reduction induced by the lower price. In reality, the actual volume increase hinges on whether the competitors react to the first price move. If they don't follow suit with their own price cuts, the volume increase will materialize; but if they do lower prices, volume is unlikely

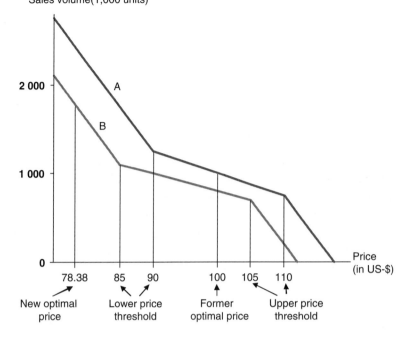

Fig. 6.3: Price-sales curve with price thresholds

Sales volume(1,000 units)

2 000   A

B

1 000

0 ────────────────────────────────── Price
         78.38   85   90   100 105 110   (in US-$)

New optimal   Lower price   Former   Upper price
   price   threshold   optimal price   threshold

to increase much. The example also shows that a very high price elasticity is required in the lower branch of the price-sales curve to offset margin decreases. Before implementing radical price cuts, a company must therefore be certain of its products' price elasticity. Reactions of competitors need to be taken into account as well. Otherwise, the entire maneuver might end in the unwarranted combination of prices that are far lower and sales volumes that have not increased.

The "scrapping bonus" for cars in Germany of $3,250[16] is a case in which the prices moved into the steep lower branch of the price-sales curve. The program is geared to subsidize the purchase of 2 million new cars in the course of 2009. Additional direct discounts from car manufacturers resulted in price cuts of up to 40%. Most consumers that qualified for the bonus belonged to lower income brackets so that these massive price reductions broke their resistance to buy a new car. Sales skyrocketed. The most recent "cash for clunkers" program in the U.S. has similar effects.[17] However, the extreme price reductions in these cases relied on massive public subsidies and thus cannot be transferred to other sectors that have to operate under normal business conditions. In a crisis, we recommend great caution before implementing large price cuts.

Quick Solution 22: Give Out Discounts in Kind, Not Price Discounts

Price concessions can be granted as reductions of the nominal price or as discounts in kind. In a crisis, discounts in kind have several advantages:

- The nominal price level remains unchanged.
- They are generally more advantageous with regard to profit than price discounts.
- They generate more volume and therefore protect jobs.

The case of an all-terrain leisure vehicle with a list price of about $10,000 serves as an excellent illustration of these advantages. As a reaction to the crisis, the manufacturer offered all dealers who ordered five vehicles a sixth unit for free. Since the dealers received six vehicles but had to pay for only five the actual price discount was 16.7%. At a price of $10,000 the results are as follows: Revenue $50,000, units sold 6, profit $14,000. If the manufacturer had given a direct price discount of 16.7% the results would have been: Revenue $41,650, units sold 5, profit $11,650. As a result of the discount in kind both the volume (and thus employment) and the profit are higher. Since the discount initiative is explicitly defined as a measure confined to the crisis, it should be easier to phase out after the crisis than a direct price discount that inevitably weakens the list price.

A manufacturer of designer furniture also reports positive outcomes from discounts in kind. This leading brand attaches great importance to price consistency. If customers demand a discount, which they do regularly and with great tenacity, an additional piece of furniture is offered for free. In most cases the customer is happy with this and does not ask for further discounts. Similar to the all-terrain vehicle-case, the results were increased employment (more products are disposed of than with direct price discounts) and higher profits. The higher profit results primarily from the different value that the manufacturer and the customer attach to the free piece of furniture. The customer sees the selling price while the manufacturer only calculates the variable costs. This means that the manufacturer can give away a piece of furniture that only costs him $60 but has a value of $100 for the customer. To give the customer the same amount in direct price discounts the manufacturer would have to forego $100.

The rental market is another area in which rebates in kind have proven superior to rent reductions. It is generally more advantageous for a landlord to grant a new tenant a few months of free rent instead of a lower rent per square foot or meter. The value of real estate is usually determined by a multiple of the rent, and banks use this benchmark when granting credit. So what matters are high monthly rents, even if they are preceded by a few months without payments. Tenants also prefer this type of rebate in kind. The reason may be that when moving into a new apartment tenants face a number of additional financial burdens such as relocation costs, purchase of new furniture, and so on.

Quick Solution 23: Deploy Non-linear Pricing and Price Bundling

Sophisticated forms of intelligent price reductions well suited for a crisis are non-linear pricing and price bundling. A further variant is multiperson pricing. With non-linear pricing, the price per unit is not constant but decreases with the number of units bought. The simplest form of non-linear pricing is the volume discount. More complex forms are two- or three-dimensional price schemes. The main difference between this method and a simple price reduction is that the customer only gets the lower price if he or she buys more.[18]

In the crisis, simple non-linear price offers have become very popular. Widely used forms are: "buy one, get one free," "two for one," "pay for two, get three," or "50 percent off the price for a second book" and so on. Such schemes help increase volume. However, the seller should exercise caution with regard to the profit impact. Such discounts are often extremely high. While they may move volume they can ruin margins.

One example of a two-dimensional, non-linear price system is the BahnCard (BC) of the German Railway Corporation. A second class BC costs $300 and a first class card costs $600.[19] With the card the customer receives a 50% discount on all tickets for one year. Thus, the average price per mile or kilometer goes down as the usage increases. The price is non-linear. Passengers who travel a lot (or, more precisely, who travel more than the breakeven volume) pay a lower total price than they would pay without the BC. For frequent railway users the BC therefore means a price reduction and an incentive to use trains more often. With every additional trip the price goes down. The BC has been a tremendous success with almost 5 million cardholders. Notice that the incentive structure is very different from a frequent flyer plan or similar bonus systems. With the BC the customer has to spend money upfront and strives to earn this money back through frequent usage. It is a very intelligent system for cutting prices and encouraging customers to buy more.

Multidimensional price systems have become very popular in sectors such as telecommunications, utilities, Internet, and services. They are also used in the industrial goods sector. One example is industrial gases where the total price consists of the lease for the container and the gas price. Depending on the duration of their consumption customers pay a completely different price per gallon or liter of gas. Flat rates are an extreme variant of non-linear pricing that has become highly popular in the last few years – especially in Internet and telecommunications services. Non-linear pricing schemes are best suited for services. These schemes can be implemented quickly and usually impact sales volume without much delay. They are particularly effective during a crisis. However, these schemes always go to the very limit of customers' willingness to pay. If these limits are overstepped profits can drop sharply. Therefore, a thorough analysis is necessary before such schemes are introduced. The profit potential of these instruments is huge, but they must be used cautiously.

While non-linear pricing is restricted to one product, price bundling includes several products. A customer who buys a pre-defined bundle or package pays a bundle price that is noticeably lower than the sum of the individual product prices. Bundling allows the seller to make price concessions that would be disadvantageous for individual products. The rationale for bundling is to transfer nonexploited willingness-to-pay for a product to the bundle. The willingness-to-pay for the bundle is less heterogeneous than for the single products, and thus can be better exploited than if the products were sold separately.[20] Well-known cases of price bundling are Microsoft's office suite or McDonald's menus. Norton, a supplier of anti-virus software, uses bundling heavily for all products. If you buy three licenses, you will get a license for another product (Norton Ghost) for free.

Figure 6.4 shows an ad for a bundle offer for Scotts lawn care products. It is eye-opening how a consumer who also happens to be a marketing expert commented on this bundle offering:[21] "I don't have a clue about how to care for my lawn, and therefore have never really looked into purchasing anything for it. But, after seeing this ad I almost felt compelled to run out and spend a few hundred dollars on lawn supplies. The key features include the following:

1. The bundle offers a complete solution. Not figuring out what my lawn needs, I just buy all these products and I'm all set.
2. Great overt cross-selling. If you had asked me what I'd be most likely to purchase for my lawn, it probably would have just been

fertilizer (step 4) and maybe crab-grass preventer (step 1). But, the way it's presented I feel like I should buy steps 2 and 3 as well.

3. Discount – If I act now, I get money off!
4. Discount is a rebate. The majority of people likely won't ever send in the rebate form – even better.
5. Subtle cross selling – I probably also "need" to buy the Scotts fertilizer spreader which is shown in the picture, but not mentioned in the total solution cost. So, my final price would probably be above the advertised price which draws me to the store."

This says it all.

Fig. 6.4: Example of an advertisement for a product bundle

During a crisis, an increase of bundling offers can indeed be observed. Again, the boundaries to rebates in kind are not clear cut. For any purchase of a new car for $29,640, a Belgian car dealer offered his customers a second car from a predefined contingent of new and used cars. During certain periods, Burger King gave a Whopper for free with every Whopper that was purchased. Similar offers exist in telecommunications. In the U.S., Verizon customers who buy a Blackberry with a 2-year contract receive a second Blackberry for free. The use of bundling is particularly interesting in the crisis as it can induce strong volume increases. The surplus volume overcompensates for the discount effect so that, despite the bundle discount, a higher profit can be achieved than by individually selling the products.

Similar to non-linear pricing, bundling can be easily implemented and is likely to have a quick and significant impact on sales and profit.

Again, a thorough analysis is required beforehand so as to fully exploit the customers' willingness to pay.

A variation of bundling is multiperson pricing, which means selling to several people at a lower price than the sum of the prices individuals would have to pay.[22] This scheme is common with tour operators (a second person or the children travel at a lower price or for free), airlines (a second person pays half price) or in the catering industry (the meal for the second person is free or is only half price). A variation of multiperson pricing was offered by Volkswagen in the spring of 2009.[23] For the Multivan United, VW granted a basic discount of $3,000 plus $2,000 for every child under 18. For a family with three children the discount amounted to $9,000.[24] Occasionally, multiperson discounts come in the form of coupon booklets. The coupons can be used by two guests in participating restaurants and only one of them has to pay; 90% of the participating restaurants say that they acquired new customers through these multiperson coupons.[25] Again, multiperson pricing leads to volume increases, can be easily implemented, and shows quick results. But, as with the schemes discussed before, caution must be exercised to avoid hurting revenues and profits.

Quick Solution 24: Defend Your Prices with Tooth and Nail

When the pressure on prices increases, one option is to give in, the other is to defend prices. There are numerous ways and means to fight against price erosion:

- Better preparation for price negotiations
- Deeper knowledge of the customer's value chain and business processes
- Quantification of customer benefits
- Clear targets and incentives
- Appointment of competent price negotiators
- Intensified monitoring of realized prices

It has been demonstrated again and again that a more professional handling of these aspects leads to improved price performance. In a recession, the ability to defend prices becomes the decisive factor, especially if the competitors defend their own sales volumes by massively lowering their prices.

In a project for one of the world's largest automotive suppliers, the pricing competence of the teams was evaluated using 15 criteria. The project found a very high correlation of 0.8 between pricing competence and realized prices. This means that higher pricing competence translates into higher margins.

A Simon-Kucher study of 56 industrial suppliers confirms that fighting against price pressure can be effective. All suppliers in the survey were facing demands from their customers in the automotive and the engineering industry to cut their prices by an average of about 5%. Figure 6.5 shows that the price cut demands of the manufacturers were more or less uniform. The outcomes, however, differed markedly. The successful suppliers had to accept price reductions of only 1.4%, whereas the less successful ones had to swallow an average price erosion of 3.8%.

The findings strongly suggest that it makes sense to stand up to price pressures. In the automotive and machinery supply industry, where margins are low even at the best of times, there is a world of difference between 1.4 and 3.8%. Under these circumstances, a price reduction of only 1.4% is a huge success.

The necessity for price defense exists in all industries. While one well-known body wear maker went bankrupt, a competitor located in the immediate neighborhood reports double-digit profit margins. How can that be? A key factor of the flourishing company's success is that it's known as being "tough" with regard to prices. Even in its factory outlet stores this company has no bargain bins indicating cheapness of the products. Instead, a general discount is given when the customer checks out. The list price of the individual product is not discounted.[26] This kind of "pricing power" is both a reflection of a

Fig. 6.5: Demanded and actual price cuts

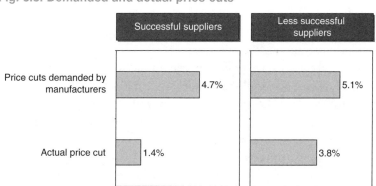

Source: Study by Simon-Kucher & Partners

brand's strength (recently the company received an award for "fastest growing product brand"), and an expression of the management's resolve to defend prices at an appropriate level. If top management stands by pricing and backs up the sales organization, a margin difference of several hundred basis points can result.[27]

Quick Solution 25: Increase Prices Under the Customers' Radar

Despite the prevailing price pressures, selective price increases can be achieved even during a crisis. There are several reasons for this. Many price systems are so complex that customers don't have price transparency. This can be due to a large product range, numerous price parameters, or complex terms and conditions. The price list of a bank, for instance, comprises several hundred positions, many of which the customer is not aware exist. Typically, customers focus on – and remember – only a few prices. Private banking customers tend to look at the monthly rates for an account, fees for their investment funds, or money market interest rates. Business customers generally know the current interest rates or the prices for transferrals. Other price parameters, such as the management fee for funds and or the debit rates for checking accounts or credit cards, are largely unknown to customers. These intransparencies open opportunities for selective price increases. Recently, a regional bank achieved immediate additional earnings of several hundred thousand dollars by selectively adjusting price components below the customers' radar. The bank received no complaints concerning the price changes. The adjustments required a careful analysis of all price and product components regarding volume (e.g., number of transactions, assets), contribution to earnings, and customer sensitivity to price increases. These aspects were analyzed quickly and cost efficiently by means of an internal survey among the sales staff.

Potential for selective price increases often exists when assortments are large. Wholesale and retail trade, spare parts, tourism, and airline travel are sectors where this condition prevails. Customers often focus on a few key items but have no idea of the prices for the rest of the assortment. This is especially true for products that are bought infrequently. What is the price of a padlock? Hardly anyone can answer this question reliably. A hobby farmer who recently needed such a padlock went into a home improvement store and found prices ranging from $4 to $12. He ended up buying a medium-priced lock for $8, a typical choice pattern if price is not known. The customer would probably have also chosen from the medium price level if the price range of the padlocks had been $4 to $16. Then he would have spent $10 instead of $8, which is a whopping 25% more. However, this procedure should not be overstretched because the price image of the store may suffer. Prices should be raised selectively, based on a detailed understanding of customers' perceptions.

Spare parts offer numerous opportunities for price increases without volume reduction. This requires that spare parts are separated into categories with varying willingness to pay and price elasticity. Two categories are exclusive parts, which can only be bought from the original manufacturer, and commodity parts, which can be bought from other manufacturers or from dealers. In a recent case, a vehicle manufacturer successfully increased the prices for spare parts by 12% and achieved a profit improvement of 20% – despite the crisis.

A very effective approach is increased price differentiation across customers. Through a detailed analysis, past transactions prices and margins can be made transparent and the main price drivers can be identified. With the help of intelligent models, the prices can be adjusted more precisely to individual customers and the full potential of the willingness to pay can be tapped. A pricing tool provides the salesforce with exact information regarding the implementation of the price differentiation. Monitoring the actual prices becomes easier and more efficient.

Quick Solution 26: Clean Out Your Discount Jungle

Selective price increases and margin improvements can be achieved by weeding out unnecessary or inconsistent discounts and by a general clearing up of "discount jungles." In many companies, discounts have spread wildly, are inconsistent, and are often too high. Many discounts are granted without a quid pro quo from the customer. Discounts tend to accumulate over time. In our projects we frequently observe that nobody can remember why and when a certain discount was accepted. Cleaning out the discount jungle can quickly and significantly improve margins.

The case in Figure 6.6 shows discounts given by a software vendor. In spite of the clearly defined guidelines for volume discounts indicated by the scaled line, no correlation could be detected between customers' sales volumes and the discounts they received. It is no exaggeration to call this a "discount jungle." It is unlikely that such a jungle is justified, let alone optimal. In our projects we frequently come across similar inconsistencies. Detection of discount jungles opens up a variety of ways to establish quick solutions for the realization of higher margins.

It is unacceptable that even small customers receive massive discounts. By simply reducing the discounts for small customers in Figure 6.6 to an appropriate level, a strong margin improvement can be achieved. This solution can be quickly implemented and has rapid and noticeable results.

Figure 6.7 reveals a typical pattern for discount negotiations; namely, the tendency to round up percentages. The case shown here is

Fig. 6.6: Discounts given by a software vendor

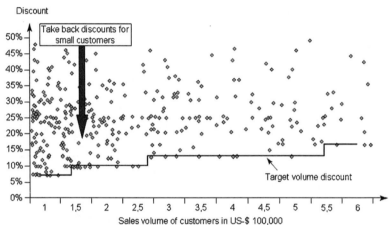

Source: Simon-Kucher & Partners

Fig. 6.7: Rounded discount levels that damage margins

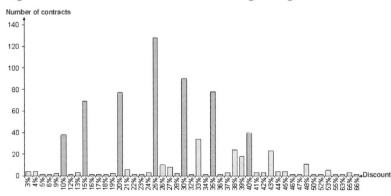

of an industrial service provider. Almost all discount percentages are round numbers, such as 10, 15 or 25%. Also, the discounts granted are very widely dispersed. If one goes to discount levels that are a few percentage points below the round figures the effects on the margin will be dramatic. The same applies to the steps between discount levels during the negotiations. Discounts are typically increased by steps of 5 or 10%. If smaller steps are applied the overall discount tends to be smaller as well.

Higher discounts might be necessary during a crisis, but the way the discounts are negotiated has a strong impact on the margins. By applying intelligent discounting, quick improvements can be achieved. In the case of a B2B company with revenues of about $5 billion the average discount was reduced by targeted measures to 14% from 16%. This amounts to a price increase of 2 percentage points and means a profit increase of $100 million. Careful and selective moves are advisable when cleaning out the discount jungle. A crisis is not the ideal time to weed out discounts. However, in our projects we have often observed that well-planned and convincingly communicated steps in that direction can be successful even in a crisis.

Quick Solution 27: Charge Separately for Hitherto Inclusive Services

A further quickly implementable method of selective price increases is charging separately for services or components that were hitherto included in a package with a single price.[28] This is the opposite of bundling and is often called unbundling. A well-known case is the low budget airline Ryanair, which introduced a separate luggage charge of $4.50 in 2006. The profit increase of 30% reported in the following quarter was largely attributed to this instance of unbundling. Once a service is charged separately the price can be repeatedly increased. Checking-in an item of luggage costs $13 with Ryanair today.[29] Additionally, low budget airlines such as Ryanair and Easyjet charge a fee for speedy boarding.

Another case is the introduction of a 50 cent fee for toilet use in motorway service areas.[30] Customers now have to pay for a hitherto free service. If they only use the toilet they contribute to the maintenance costs. Customers who make purchases in the shop or restaurant can cash in the 50 cent token. The majority of customers make use of this possibility, which strongly increases cross-selling. In other cases, the introduction of a separate price failed. A spectacular case was the attempt of the German Railroad corporation to introduce a service charge of $3.25 or 2.50 Euros for tickets bought from a salesperson at the counter – as opposed to tickets purchased on the Internet or a ticket machine. A storm of indignation broke out and the plan had to be shelved. In another case, a low cost airport (a former U.S. airbase) attempted to collect a service fee of $4 from each passenger. Like the German Railroad scheme, this price structure also met with resistance and failed. With 4 million passengers a year this would have meant additional earnings of $16 million for this airport, not a negligible sum. In the spring of 2009, Ryanair announced that it is considering a fee for toilet use during flights, a plan that might meet the same fate as German Rail's service charge or the airport service fee.

Separately charging for components formerly included in the price is not only restricted to services but can be applied to products as well. An interesting example is the television function in the BMW 7-series. In first generation navigation systems this function was included without surcharge. From the second generation on it was offered as a separate feature. Today, the TV function costs more than $2,000.[31] Once separate prices are established, prices can adjust over the life-cycle of a model. In contrast to technical adjustments, no model change is necessary. At the most, the price list needs to be reprinted.

The crisis may not be the ideal time to start charging separately for services and products. Everything depends on the customers' reaction. Will they accept the surcharge as in the case of Ryanair, motorway toilet usage, and BMW, or will there be strong negative reactions as with the train tickets or the airport? It is necessary to consider and test these reactions beforehand. Ryanair, for example, reasoned that the luggage charge actually amounted to a price advantage for passengers who don't check in any luggage. If the services can be clearly separated and possibly even improved (as in the motorway toilet case) customer acceptance can be achieved even during a crisis.

All these cases – be it the selective increase of individual parameters or articles, the differentiation between customers, or unbundling – require very detailed information. All these measures approach the limits of customers' willingness to pay. Mistakes can lead to drastic customer reactions. To achieve the delicate balance, profound knowledge of price elasticities, that is, the relationship between price and volume, is required. This kind of information can be obtained through systematic studies, in management workshops, or through careful experimentation in the market.

Even in good times, there is widespread fear of price increases and the ensuing volume losses among managers. During a crisis such fears multiply. When business is bad the prospect of further revenue declines can cause panicked reactions. These are not the ideal conditions to achieve optimal results, to implement price increases, or to fight against price pressure. In a crisis, top management must back up the sales team and alleviate their fear of price negotiations.

Not a Quick Solution: Price Wars

We do not consider avoiding price wars as a quick solution, since it's not about doing something but rather about not doing something. However, refraining from engaging in price wars can make the difference between survival and demise. In a crisis, demand falls. The fight for market shares and revenues becomes even tougher than before. A single company can only maintain its absolute sales volume if it takes away market share from competitors. This is worse than a zero-sum game, it's a negative sum game. Striving to increase market share by means of overly aggressive pricing leads to competitive retaliation. The worst-case scenario is a price war that ruins the margins and profits of all competitors. The danger of a price war increases sharply during a crisis. Overcapacities and low demand are seen as the main causes of price wars.[32] Everything should be done to avoid price wars during a crisis unless a company has the financial strength to eliminate a weakened opponent in a short period of time. The most important guidelines in this regard are as follows:

- In a crisis, an orientation towards market share and volume should be replaced by a rigorous profit and cash flow orientation.
- Companies should aim at peaceful competition that gives all competitors the ability to guard their margins.
- Aggressive price actions should be avoided. Signaling and communication should be targeted towards this goal.
- Submarkets that are unattractive and where a company is weak should be conceded to competitors. Areas of conflict should be avoided.
- It is important to bring the whole organization behind the rigorous profit orientation. One way of doing this is to set profit-oriented targets and incentives for the management and the salesforce.

Experience shows that these suggestions often lead to heated discussions in everyday business. Despite the crisis, overly aggressive attitudes prevail in some companies causing unnecessary dangers.

Summary

Since a crisis is characterized by an imbalance between supply and demand, managing offers and prices plays a central role in successfully coping with the economic environment. The following points should be noted:

- Volume and capacity should be limited to take the pressure off the market and stabilize prices.
- Efforts should be made to achieve an industry-wide volume reduction. The rules of conduct for oligopolistic markets should be observed.
- Supply should be reduced in connection with the price decision and taking into account the price-sales curve.
- It is important to quantify these interrelations as precisely as possible. Even small changes in the price-sales curve can lead to large differences in the optimal price-volume combination.
- Price reductions are often unavoidable in a crisis. It is important to achieve the highest possible positive effect on sales when prices are cut. This may require going below price thresholds and enhancing price communication.
- Discounts in kind tend to be superior to direct price discounts.
- More professional preparation, negotiation, and monitoring can help to stabilize prices.
- Despite the crisis, selective price increases should be considered and realized. Chances are best with price components that remain below the customers' radar and with increased price differentiation between customers.
- Separately charging for formerly inclusive services can be a way to achieve higher profits despite the crisis.
- Price wars should be avoided in a crisis, unless a company has the financial strength to eliminate an opponent in a short period of time.

The numerous approaches and cases in this chapter show that, despite the crisis, all is not lost. The management of offers and prices presents many opportunities to beat the crisis and to save revenue and profit. Solid information and the will to act are all it takes.

Endnotes

1 "Freude am Sparen," *Focus Money*, February 4, 2009, p. 76.

2 "U.S. Industrial Production Drops More Than Forecast," bloomberg.com, April 15, 2009.

3 "Nach Ostern beginnt wieder das normale Leben," Interview with Burkhard Weller, founder of car dealer Autoweller, *Frankfurter Allgemeine Zeitung*, March 9, 2009, p. 15.

4 "Dow Chemical to Cut 5,000 Jobs," cnnmoney.com, December 8, 2008.

5 *The Wall Street Journal*, June 12, 2009, p. B1.

6 Hermann Simon and Martin Fassnacht, *Preismanagement*, third edition, Wiesbaden: Gabler 2009.

7 Klaus Meitinger, "Wege aus der Krise," *Private Wealth*, March 2009, pp. 26–31.

8 Geoff Colvin, "Yes, You Can Raise Prices," *Fortune*, March 2, 2009, p. 19.

9 In linear price–sales curves the optimal price is in the middle between variable unit costs (here $60) and the maximum or reservation price, that is, the point of intersection of the price–sales curve and the price axis. In the left case the maximum price is $140, in the right case $132 (cf. Hermann Simon and Martin Fassnacht, *Preismanagement*, third edition, Wiesbaden: Gabler 2009).

10 Statement made in September 2003 during the International Automotive Fair in Frankfurt.

11 In a personal conversation with the author, Georg Tacke, Senior Partner at Simon-Kucher & Partners, reported this statement by Wendelin Wiedeking.

12 "Sportwagenhersteller Porsche muss sparen," *Frankfurter Allgemeine Zeitung*, January 31, 2009, p. 14.

13 Robert J. Dolan and Hermann Simon, *Power Pricing*, New York: Free Press 1996, Hermann Simon and Martin Fassnacht, *Preismanagement*, third edition, Wiesbaden: Gabler 2009.

14 Robert J. Dolan and Hermann Simon, *Power Pricing*, New York: Free Press 1996.

15 The price elasticity is defined as the change in sales volume in percent (here: 125%) divided by the change in price in percent (here: 22%). It is a negative figure because a price reduction has positive effects on sales (and vice versa).

16 The scrapping bonus was 2,500 Euros, which at an exchange rate of $1.30 per euro corresponds to $3,250.

17 The subsidy is between $3,500 and $4,500; see *Time*, August 17, 2009, p. 8.

18 For a more detailed description of non-linear pricing, cf. Georg Tacke, *Nichtlineare Preisbildung*, Wiesbaden: Gabler 1989.

19 Prices in $ are rounded. Actual prices in Euros are 225 for the second class and 450 for the first class BahnCard. At an exchange rate of $1.30 per Euro, this results in the approximate $-prices.

20 For a more detailed description of price bundling, cf. Georg Wübker, *Preisbündelung*: Formen, Theorien, Messung und Umsetzung, Wiesbaden: Gabler 1998, and Georg Wübker, *Power Pricing für Banken*, second edition, Frankfurt: Campus 2008.

21 E-mail to the author from consultant Dr. Nathan Swilling, Boston, March 23, 2009.

22 Hermann Simon and Georg Wübker, "Mehr-Personen-Preisbildung: Eine neue Form der Preisdifferenzierung mit beachtlichem Gewinnsteigerungspotenzial," *Zeitschrift für Betriebswirtschaft*, 2000, pp. 729–746.

23 *Welt am Sonntag*, March 15, 2009, p. 11.

24 $-figures are rounded; the exact amounts in Euros were 2,365 Euros base discount plus 1,500 Euros per child.

25 "Kulinarische Kostverächter," *Frankfurter Allgemeine Zeitung*, March 5, 2009, p. 19.

26 "Ohne Wühltische an die Wäsche gehen," *Frankfurter Allgemeine Zeitung*, March 10, 2009, p. 17.

27 A basis point is a term from financial economics and means one hundredth of 1%.

28 For a more profound description, cf. Frank Bilstein and Sebastian Voigt, "Früher war das doch umsonst?", *Absatzwirtschaft*, March 2009, pp. 40–42.

29 $-prices rounded, exchange rate $1.30 per Euro. Ryanair's actual luggage charges in Euro were 3.50 Euros in 2006 and 10 Euros in 2009.

30 This fee was introduced in 2008 by Tank & Rast, the company operating motorway service areas in Germany.

31 The price of the TV function in Germany in 2009 was 1,650 Euros corresponding to $2,145 at an exchange rate of $1.30 per Euro. Cf. price list of BMW 7-series, manufacturers homepage (http://www.bmw.de), March 11, 2009.

32 Hermann Simon, Frank Bilstein and Frank Luby, *Manage for Profit, Not for Market Share*, Boston: Harvard Business School Press 2006.

Chapter 7
Quick Solutions for Services

Services are not only offered by "typical" service providers such as hotels, airlines or banks. Industrial companies also generate a considerable part of their revenues from services. Services such as maintenance, repair, refurbishing, and spare parts often account for 20% of the revenue of industrial firms and for an even higher percentage of their profits. Services, including spare parts, usually achieve higher margins than new products. The results of a study among mechanical engineering companies shown in Figure 7.1 reflect large differences in the profit margins.

During the boom years, services have been neglected compared to the new product business. This is hardly surprising. When facing manufacturing and supply bottlenecks and tight delivery schedules, managers inevitably and rightly focus on production and delivery issues. In a "seller's market" add-on services move to the backseat. This implies that untapped revenue and profit potentials are hidden in the service realm. The current underemployment on the production front suggests turning management attention to services.

If a company has a large installed base,[1] the service and spare parts business is typically much less sensitive to crises and recessions than the new product business. This is illustrated by the case of Demag Cranes, one of the global market leaders in industrial and harbor cranes. Orders for harbor cranes plummeted by 39% during the first quarter of the business year 2008/2009 while those for industrial cranes still grew slightly by 3%. Service orders, on the other hand, grew robustly by 9.4%. Figure 7.2 shows the changes in order inflow.

"Even in a prolonged recession, harbor installations need maintenance," says the CEO of Demag Cranes.[2] One reason for the increase in service orders are the efforts of Demag Cranes to sign service contracts with as many customers as possible. Of Demag's revenue of $1.2 billion, 26.8% come from services. Behind this is a huge installed base of 650,000 cranes, 50% of which are serviced by Demag.

H. Simon, *Beat the Crisis: 33 Quick Solutions for Your Company*,
DOI 10.1007/978-1-4419-0823-0_7, © Hermann Simon 2010

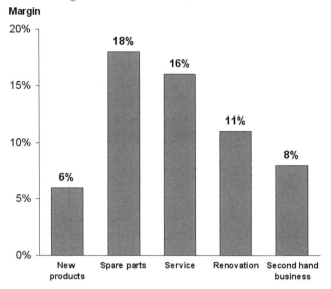
Fig. 7.1: Profit margins achieved in different businesses

Source: Study by Simon-Kucher & Partners among 76 mechanical engineering companies

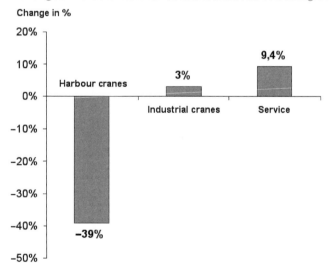
Fig. 7.2: Changes in order inflow for different divisions of Demag Cranes

Demag's main competitor, Konecranes from Finland, generates as much as 36% of its revenue through services. With a service revenue of almost $1 billion Konecranes is the global number one in this business. Konecranes calls itself a "full service provider" and offers "premium class service" independent of the manufacturer of the crane. The company has more than 360,000 service contracts for cranes in 43 countries, a large part of which is for products by other manufacturers. Konecranes sees the service business not merely as an extension of its own product business but as a standalone activity.

A high share of services can considerably lower business risks and soften the impact of the crisis. Services are less cyclical than new product sales. This is particularly true for products such as cranes, lifts, power stations, and so on, for which legal service intervals exist. In addition, other companies like Xerox report that its multiyear contracts for document services help it to cope with the crisis.[3] There are many more approaches to stimulate the business with services and spare parts. We will discuss them in the following pages.

A simple way to generate additional revenue is to charge separately for services that were formerly included in the total price. Industrial companies typically offer numerous services that are included in the product price and not invoiced separately. Unbundling these services from the overall package and charging separately for them can have considerable effects on revenue and profit. The higher margins shown in Fig. 7.1 contribute to this improvement. Unbundling needs to be handled with great caution however, especially in the crisis. There are many industries with long traditions of inclusive services that have never been separately billed. The reaction of customers who notice that they suddenly have to pay extra for such services can be very negative. On the other hand, we often observe in our projects that separate charges are accepted if they apply to a service that is considered extraordinary or above the usual standard. Examples are express charges, surcharges for lower quantities or special training courses, unusual guarantees or the assumption of risks by the vendor.

Quick Solution 28: Extend Your Value Chain by Enhanced Service Offerings

If a company has not yet offered services but there is a demand for service among its customers, there is an opportunity to soften the negative effects of the crisis. A case in point is Media-Saturn, Europe's leading retailer for consumer electronics, with revenues of $25 billion. So far, Media-Saturn had only offered a restricted range of services. With the onset of the crisis, it started to test the introduction of a service program called "Powerservice 24." In this program all services are offered at fixed prices. The services include delivery and installation, optimization and maintenance, computer services and the solution of technical problems for all devices. If the test shows positive results, introduction in all stores is planned.

Such extensions of the depth of the service value chain require additional personnel. Often employees who are not fully employed due to the crisis but who are familiar with the products can perform the new services. Similar to the deployment of internal staff to sales, there are two advantages. One is that these employees generate additional revenue through their services; the other is a positive effect on the working climate since fewer people sit idle at their desks. Gartner Research predicts an extension of services by mobile carriers towards content transmitted to the end customer instead of just providing the infrastructure for third-party providers.[4] Similar extensions can be applied for different industries with service potential.

Industrial and trading companies (such as retailers) frequently offer only a limited range of services and don't fully utilize the inherent opportunities. A large manufacturer of prefabricated houses with an installed base of several thousand houses only reacts to customers' service requests, but does not actively offer its services. This is not what one would call a customer-oriented service strategy. Since services require different forms of organization and leadership than a factory, manufacturers often regard them as an annoying duty, not as a business opportunity. With such anti-service attitudes, companies are foregoing revenues, which is dangerous and unacceptable during a severe crisis.

On the other hand, there are manufacturers who offer comprehensive services and thus generate both high and margin-enhancing service revenues. For example, wind turbine manufacturer Enercon guarantees its customers a continuously high availability of its wind power plants for the first twelve years. All contingencies from maintenance and safety to repairs are covered by one single service contract. The Enercon Partner Concept (EPC) meets with great customer approval; more than 85% of them sign a 12-year contract. The rapidly growing "installed base" makes Enercon less susceptible to crises and recessions.

One extension of the value chain consists of training for customers. Training becomes more and more important as a service. Reasons are the increasing complexity of products, as well as the move into countries in which the education level of employees who are supposed to use sophisticated products is rather low, for example, emerging countries. Some companies have special business units for their training activities, which makes separate billing easier. Festo, world market leader in pneumatic automation technology, has founded Festo Didactic, which calls itself the "worldwide leader in professional, industry-oriented qualification solutions for process and factory automation" and offers training courses in more than 100 countries. The contents of the trainings are of a broad range, not limited to Festo products and also directed at non-customers of Festo products. During the crisis, courses that lead to quick cost savings are particularly popular. How quickly extensions of the service value chain can be implemented depends on the specific competencies required.

Quick Solution 29: Increase the Share of Customers with Service Contracts

Intensified sales initiatives can significantly increase the share of customers who buy a service contract. This is again illustrated by the example of Demag Cranes. By winning over new service customers the company increased the revenue share coming from services from 18.4% in 2005/2006 to 26.8% in 2007/2008. This is an increase of 46% in only 2 years, which means additional revenues of about $200 million per year for Demag.

A similar way has been chosen by Cisco, the world-leading manufacturer of routers and interfaces for Internet dataflow. In the crisis, Cisco increasingly uses services to keep growing and to stabilize revenues. While order inflow for products declined 20% in January 2009, revenues from services increased 10% compared to the year before.[5] At Hewlett Packard, the service sector is also growing more rapidly than the other parts of the company. While most of its divisions stagnated, HP Services grew by 5.6%.

Quick Solution 30: Change from Product to Systems Provider

The crisis does not only affect competitors but also complementary suppliers as well as upstream and downstream vendors. This presents opportunities to become a systems provider instead of a mere product provider. Groz-Beckert, world market leader in textile needles, for example, transformed itself from a manufacturer of knitting and hosiery needles to a comprehensive systems provider for precision parts. Business was extended to sewing machines, felting, structuring and tufting needles, as well as to parts for weaving machines. In this last sector, the global leader in weaving machine parts, Grob Horgen, and the German company Schmeing were acquired. However, the transition from product to systems provider can take some time, so this approach is not always suitable for short-term crisis management.

Hako, one of the global market leaders in professional cleaning machines, generates only 20% of its revenues from selling machines. A much larger revenue share comes from a comprehensive solution package consisting of leasing, service, object planning, and advice. Hako offers its customers programs to calculate the requirements for their objects and guarantees the calculated costs, thereby sharing the customers' entrepreneurial risk. As managing director Bernd Heilmann points out, Hako is no longer an industrial company, but "a service provider for service providers" with a comprehensive systems offering.

Lantal, world market leader in customized cabin interiors for commercial airplanes, provides airlines with a comprehensive systems package consisting of the interior design along specific customer wishes, as well as the production of seat covers, curtains, wall coverings, headrests and carpets.[6] But Lantal extended this systems offer even further. Based on the insight that cabin interiors have to fulfill very strict safety regulations, Lantal has applied for and received authorization from the European Aviation Safety Agency (EASA) and the American Federal Aviation Administration (FAA) to certify fabrics and carpets. In complex certification and liability matters, customers definitely prefer to deal with one supplier instead of several.

An additional effect of the systems offer is increased customer retention. Studies have shown that customers who buy several products or entire systems from one company change suppliers less frequently than customers who buy only one product. This side effect is highly welcome because it adds to the stability of a business.

Quick Solution 31: Increase Your Service Flexibility

The flexibility and availability of service can be an important issue in the crisis. An English company recently snatched the carpet order for a luxury hotel from a German carpet manufacturer. The German company was unable to lay the carpets in the extremely short period of time requested by the hotel. The employees of the English company worked around the clock as well as on weekends. The order for a huge solar plant with an investment volume of $33 million went to the installation company that was able to fulfil the order the quickest. The investor had to get the plant operational before the end of the year to receive the higher feeding price, which ran out at the end of 2008. The plant was finished in time only because the service company worked around the clock and on weekends, and in spite of adverse weather conditions. During the crisis, employees and unions are more willing to accept such flexible solutions that are more demanding on the workers than in good times. In the crisis, flexibility and speed count even more than under normal circumstances.

Quick Solution 32: Shift Your Focus from the Original Market to the Aftermarket

When we talk about a drop in sales during the crisis, we refer almost always to the original market. Markets for used products can even profit in the crisis as customers increasingly look for ways to acquire products cheaply. In the current crisis, the original markets for "postponables" have collapsed on a wide front. This applies to cars as well as to domestic appliances, furniture, consumer electronics, and home construction. The same is true for industrial products such as machines or plant equipment. However, in many of the affected sectors sales are not confined to the original market, and the aftermarket contributes a considerable share to revenues, even during normal times. Car tires are not only needed for new cars but also as replacements for worn tires. The aftermarket for tires is actually three times the size of the original market. In Europe, of a total of 368 million tires, 91 million were sold on the original market and 277 million on the aftermarket in 2008. A similar structure applies for heating systems. With an assumed life cycle of 20 years, 5% of all heating systems have to be exchanged every year.

If the original market collapses in the crisis, the obvious solution is to direct more resources to the aftermarket in order to compensate at least partially for revenue losses. Ian Robertson, BMW's executive vice president of sales, says, "We should try to lure more owners of old cars into our garages. This is an important part of our strategy 'number one.' So far our garages concentrated mainly on the owners of recent models. Many owners of cars that were four years old or older went to car repair chains or independent garages. This is going to change."[7]

That this strategy works is corroborated by the spare parts business. The fact that consumers are not buying new cars and instead drive their old cars longer has brought robust revenue and profit growth to spare parts providers despite the crisis. AutoZone, number one in the American market and ranked 394 on the Fortune 500 List, reported a sales growth of 8% and a profit growth of 9% for the last quarter of 2008.[8]

Insula Terra,[9] a manufacturer of insulation materials, reacted to the drop in new construction activity by refocusing its business on the renovation of old buildings. The increased interest in saving energy has strongly improved the prospects in this market. Insula Terra has also adjusted its public relations and advertising activities to this submarket.

With the manufacturer of prefabricated houses we mentioned earlier, new orders have gone down sharply. Although having an installed base of several thousand houses, this manufacturer did not actively offer services. As a reaction to the crisis, the company has now started to sell services actively. These services range from simple repairs to comprehensive modernizations aimed at saving energy. The new service orders can easily be handled by the qualified but underemployed workers from the factory and the installation teams.

A smart selling process can help to fully exploit the opportunities in the aftermarket. The methods of cross-selling and bundling, which we discussed in earlier chapters, can be employed to establish a stronger connection between original and aftermarket purchases. An attractive bundle of product and services can markedly increase the share of customers who buy a service contract. This leads to higher and less volatile service revenues and profits.[10]

Quick Solution 33: Develop Innovative Service Offers

Service innovations can often be realized much more quickly than product innovations, and are therefore particularly suitable to fight the crisis. Sometimes a service innovation simply consists of bundling services that were hitherto sold individually into a package and selling them at a fixed price. Such solutions can be quickly implemented.

A comprehensive problem solution by one single provider means more convenience, safety and efficiency for the customer. The Australian company Orica, world market leader in commercial explosives, offers quarry operators a comprehensive blasting solution. Orica not only supplies the explosives, but analyzes the rocks, and carries out the drilling and the blasting. In this business model, Orica supplies the customer with broken rocks and charges accordingly. Since this model is customer-specific, the price becomes less transparent and the revenue per customer as well as efficiency and safety increase. The customer no longer worries about the blasting process, which makes it harder for him to bail out. A change to another supplier becomes more difficult.

The company Giebeler normally builds large oil tanks, made-to-measure, for its customers. In its region, Giebeler has so far installed more than 20,000 tanks. As business with new tanks started to slow down in the crisis, Giebeler needed work and came up with the idea of a standardized, all-over renovation of the installed oil tanks. This special offer includes cleaning, the elimination of mud residue, the disposal of cleaning materials, renewal of the inner tank coatings, and a 5-year guarantee. Before the house owner places an order with Giebeler a free safety check of the tank is available. This service package is offered at a fixed price based on variable components such as liter or cubic meter of removed mud residue or wall coating. Such an innovative offer needs to be clearly communicated to potential customers. To do this, Giebeler uses leaflets with very detailed information, including the introduction of individual employees with a photo and a brief profile. In the leaflets the company's tradition of more than a hundred years service is heavily stressed. These leaflets are dropped into the mailboxes of the customers whose addresses Giebeler knows from the original installation of the tanks – an efficient way to communicate the service offer directly to the target group, minimizing wastage.

Kmart, a part of Sears Holdings, Wal-Mart, Best Buy, and others are extending their service business to a "marriage between online shopping and bricks and mortar," especially on fresh food. Although not a brand-new idea, the traditional chain operators try to increase their share of the e-commerce pie, especially in regions with lower population density, by a cost-efficient and customer-oriented site-to-store concept (order online and pick up on-site).[11] B2B companies also upgrade their service quality by introducing online monitoring systems. These systems allow for continuous monitoring, thus recognizing problems immediately and achieving higher uptime of systems.[12]

We previously mentioned BMW's intention to lure more owners of older cars into its own garages. Head of sales Ian Robertson says, "We have put together lucrative service packages. We are even offering refurbished spare parts which are a lot cheaper than original spares."[13] This is an unusual and truly innovative service offer for a premium car manufacturer such as BMW. In a test in a large city, almost 400 new service customers were won with this innovative service within a month.

Generally, services offered at fixed prices or flat rates are rapidly growing. In a time of crisis in which customers are less willing to take risks these approaches are effective ways to generate additional revenue. While flat rate offers have almost become the norm in telecommunications today, there are still sectors in which such service offers are rare and considered very innovative. An example is the cinema chain CinemaX, which recently introduced a flat rate that allows customers to watch movies in any CinemaX movie theater as often as they like during the six or twelve months the card is valid. Mercedes, Ford, and other car manufacturers are offering complete-service packages for new cars, which cover all normal maintenance and repair costs for the duration of the leasing contract.

Summary

During the boom years many companies neglected the development of services. Services are generally less sensitive to crises and recessions than product sales. During the crisis, this implies opportunities to compensate for declining revenue by focusing more strongly on the service business. The main ideas from this chapter are as follows:

- In services, profit margins are usually higher than in the product business. Therefore, focusing on services implies not only additional revenues but disproportionally higher margins.
- A large installed base is an excellent way to achieve considerable service revenues.
- The value chain can be extended by offering additional services. This generates increased revenues and new jobs for underemployed personnel.
- Existing service offers should be enriched. Service offers should be more actively communicated to the customers.
- Often, only a small percentage of the customers sign service contracts. Increasing this percentage is an effective way to improve and stabilize revenues.

- By changing from product provider to systems and service provider, a company can considerably extend its business and, at the same time, achieve higher customer retention.
- During the crisis, the flexibility and instant availability of services are increasingly important. Disadvantages created by a lack of service flexibility must be avoided.
- In a stagnating or shrinking original market, shifting the focus to the aftermarket can soften or even compensate for revenue losses.
- The lead times for service innovations are typically shorter than for product innovations. Many new service offers can be quickly implemented to generate rapid additional revenue.
- By bundling existing services and supplying them at fixed prices or flat rates virtual new service offerings can be created.

Many manufacturers remain skeptical and inert with regard to new or extended service offers. In the crisis, such an attitude is unacceptable. By conceiving and offering services more effectively, revenue and profit can be quickly improved. The development and implementation of new services require both creativity and pragmatism.

Endnotes

1 Installed base refers to the accumulated number of units of a durable product or system actually in use. Because installed base includes products that may have been in use for many years, it is usually a much higher number than the annual sales volume.

2 "Demag Cranes im Abschwung," *Frankfurter Allgemeine Zeitung*, February 11, 2009, p. 14.

3 "Xerox Stock Soars 20%," cnnmoney.com, November 24, 2008.

4 "Gartner Says Carriers Will Struggle to Maintain Market Position Without Major Innovation and Change," gartner.com, April 14, 2009.

5 "Cisco Aims to Serve," *Fortune,* March 16, 2009, and "Schwaches Ergebnis, düstere Aussichten," Manager-Magazin.de, February 5, 2009.

6 "Wohnlichkeit in der Flugzeugkabine," *Neue Zürcher Zeitung*, February 5, 2007, p. 7.

7 "Kein offenes Scheckbuch," Wirtschaftswoche, February 19, 2009, p. 12.

8 "In the Zone," *Fortune,* April 20, 2009, pp. 61–62.

9 Name disguised for confidentiality reasons.

10 For examples see Hermann Simon, *Preismanagement,* second edition, Wiesbaden: Gabler 1992, p. 451.

11 "Order Online, Pick Up at the Drive-Through," ft.com, January 27, 2009.

12 "GE Healthcare Supports Customer Uptime via Remote Services," webwire. com, April 7, 2009.

13 "Kein offenes Scheckbuch," *Wirtschaftswoche*, February 19, 2009, p. 12.

Chapter 8

Implementing the Quick Solutions

Perhaps the gravest mistake in hazardous times is to stand by helplessly believing that the crisis will take its toll anyway. The 33 quick solutions and the numerous case studies described in the previous chapters demonstrate that companies are not defenseless against the crisis but can successfully tackle it. Siemens CEO Peter Loescher warns against resignation, "We managers have to put all our strength into fighting the crisis with confidence. We must not confine ourselves to saying that we don't know what's ahead and that we see nothing but a wall of fog."[1] To get the best out of difficult circumstances, companies have to pull out all the stops and mobilize the three profit drivers: cost, price, and sales volume. A wide array of methods and instruments are available: flexible cost-cutting instead of mass firings, adapting to customers' changing needs, mobilizing the sales energies, limiting supply, streamlining the product line, more sophisticated price structures, creative services, and many more. When it comes to diagnosis, decisions, and implementation, speed is of the essence. For many companies it's a matter of survival. Solutions that won't work for a year or two are of little value in face of the imminent danger.

Avoiding Major Mistakes

But no matter how pressing the issues, it is crucial to avoid making fatal mistakes.[2] We hear time and again that the crisis harbors tremendous opportunities for companies that act quickly and decisively. This may be true, but it also harbors the risk of making fatal mistakes. In a recent discussion with the CEO of a company that had just celebrated its 100th birthday the question was asked how companies manage to survive for 100 years or longer – a rare achievement in the real economy.[3] This CEO offered a number of incisive views about the possible reasons: a long-term orientation, conservative financing, reticence

H. Simon, *Beat the Crisis: 33 Quick Solutions for Your Company*,
DOI 10.1007/978-1-4419-0823-0_8, © Hermann Simon 2010

about management trends, leadership continuity, and other aspects. In particular, however, he stressed the importance of avoiding major mistakes. This CEO did not believe that long-lived companies were smarter or had better strategic insights than the others. Perhaps, he said, they simply avoid the mistakes that other companies make, or act more quickly to correct inadvertent errors. Summing up, he stated, "You don't have to be clever to be successful, but you mustn't be stupid."[4] During a crisis, this advice is more fitting than ever. When times are good a company can survive with certain mistakes, or can counterbalance them. But when a company is on the edge of disaster, every wrong move can seal its fate. In the summer of 2008, then healthy INA Schaeffler, one of the world leaders in ball bearings, took over the much bigger Continental, one of the world's leading automotive suppliers. This daring move may not have turned into a threat during a boom, but once the crisis set in the debt of almost $30 billion taken on by INA became into a millstone around the company's neck.

Striking the right balance between speed of implementation and avoiding mistakes is also a big issue in the various macroeconomic crisis programs. According to Christina Romer, chairwoman of President Obama's Council of Economic Advisors, "It's all about timing." Her view is that policy programs failed in the past because they came too late. Professor John B. Taylor of Stanford University, on the other hand, doubts that speed should receive top priority: "The idea that all we need is speed should be questioned based even on very recent experience."[5] Obviously, the need to act quickly and achieve a rapid impact conflicts with the avoidance of making serious errors. The challenge is to find the right balance between the two.

The most crucial errors to be avoided during the crisis are as follows:

1. Lax liquidity management
2. Hasty, impulsive action without understanding
3. Massive price cuts
4. Indiscriminate mass layoffs
5. Confinement to only one profit driver
6. Solutions that cost money in the short term but only have long-term effects

Evaluating the Quick Solutions

Chapters 4–7 outlined 33 quick solutions for beating the crisis. Normally, a company would not implement all of them but would choose the most appropriate ones depending on the business model, the product, the market and the competitive situation, and on how much the solution will cost. It is advisable not to reject any solutions from the outset, but to assess the suitability of each one in turn. Figure 8.1 has been designed to help with this assessment. It can be used to evaluate the 33 quick solutions with regard to their general feasibility, speed of implementation, strength, and speed of effect on sales, cost, profit, and risk. Further criteria, such as the strength and speed of the liquidity impact and the time that costs will be incurred, can be added. Figure 8.1 implies the impact on liquidity, which results primarily from the effect on sales, costs, and profit contribution. Depending on the situation, these and other aspects can be of importance and should therefore be taken into account.

Figure 8.1 is intended not as a universally applicable tool but to help companies decide which quick solutions to adopt. The recommended method is to assess each solution using a scale from 1 to 10, with 10 representing the best case (very high sales impact, very low costs, etc.). These scores can then simply be added to create an overall score for each quick solution.

Figure 8.1 illustrates the concrete evaluation for one quick solution from each area. With 52 points, quick solution 32 (Shift your focus from the original market to the aftermarket) achieves the highest total score in the set of solutions considered here. Quick solution 5

Fig. 8.1: Overview and evaluation of the quick solutions

Quick solution		General feasibility (high = 10)	Speed of implementation (high = 10)	Effect on sales		Costs (low = 10)	Profit contribution (high = 10)	Risk (low = 10)	Overall evaluation (total)
				Strength (high = 10)	Speed (high = 10)				
Customers	1. Offer extended warranties!								
	2. Arrange trial periods for machines!								
	3. Accept success-dependent payments!								
	4. Communicate tangible benefits!								
	5. Capitalize on your financial strength!	5	7	5	6	3	5	2	33
	6. Accept barter-trades!								
	7. Lure customers away from weakened competitors!								
	8. Develop new business models!								
Sales and Sales Force	9. Boost your company's sales performance!								
	10. Increase your core sales time!								
	11. Visit customers more selectively!								
	12. Strengthen direct sales!								
	13. Penetrate new customer segments!								
	14. Offer special incentives!								
	15. Redeploy in-house staff to the sales force!								
	16. Lure sales people away from competitors!								
	17. Mobilize top sales excellence!								
	18. Step up cross-selling!	7	5	6	7	8	8	7	48
	19. Expand your sales portfolio!								
Offers and Prices	20. Cut your volume!								
	21. Cut prices intelligently!								
	22. Give out discounts in kind, not price discounts								
	23. Deploy non-linear pricing and price bundling!								
	24. Defend your prices with tooth and nail!								
	25. Increase prices under the customer's radar!	9	6	2	4	10	6	2	39
	26. Clean out your discount jungle!								
	27. Charge separately for hitherto included services!								
Service and Performance	28. Extend your value chain with enhanced service offers!								
	29. Increase the number of customers with service contracts!								
	30. Change from product to systems provider!								
	31. Increase your service flexibility!								
	32. Shift your focus from the original market to the aftermarket!	9	7	8	7	7	7	7	52
	33. Develop innovative service offers!								

(Capitalize on your financial strength) has a total score of only 33; its high costs and risk make it much less suitable in this case. In the mid-range are the quick solutions 18 (Step up cross-selling) and 25 (Increase prices under the customer's radar) with 48 and 39 points, respectively. We want to remind the reader that these evaluations have to be done for each individual case. There is no general quick solution. The evaluation method can be refined by weighting the various criteria, but usually the rough method described here will suffice. The purpose at this stage is to make an initial selection of quick solutions before going into greater implementation details.

The Implementation Process

Once a company has chosen which of the quick solutions to pursue further, it needs to answer seven questions:

1. *What exactly is to be done?*
Example: What shall we offer as a discount in kind? The same product, or something else from our product line?
2. *How much?*
Example: How much counter-value should we offer as a discount in kind? 10, 15, or 20%? Subject to what conditions (e.g., minimum purchase amount)?
3. *How will the solution be implemented internally?*
Example: General rule or case-by-case decision? Where will the discount be booked (by profit center, as overhead, by region, by salesperson)?
4. *Who will be responsible?*
Example: Top management, sales management, individual salesperson?
5. *How will the solution be communicated?*
Example: Openly/actively or reactively? In the media? Face-to-face?
6. *What will be the solution's impact on sales, margin, revenue, costs, profits and liquidity?*
Example: Sales gain of 3%.
7. *How soon will the impact be felt?*
Example: Within three months.

These questions need to be considered carefully in order to reach a well-founded decision and keep the risk of mistakes to a minimum. Figure 8.2 illustrates this process taking the example of a B2B project. It contains the answers to the seven questions for the quick solutions chosen. In this case, six solutions were selected using the process from Fig. 8.1.

Instant and Parallel Action

All of the quick solutions must be implemented quickly and resolutely. In normal times, the implementation process follows a systematic sequence: situation analysis, decision, implementation, and monitoring/ controlling. In a crisis, however, urgency dictates that the process be modified. The author recommends a procedure similar to simultaneous engineering, with some of the steps being implemented in parallel.[6] Figure 8.3 provides an illustration of such a process.

For solution 1, it is possible to make a quick diagnosis and a rapid decision, immediately followed by the implementation. Solution 2,

Fig. 8.2: Implementing the selected quick solutions

Solution	To do?	How much?	Implementation?	Who is responsible?	Communication?	Expected impact?	How quickly?
3. Accept success-dependent payments	Service A is suitable; success can be quantified	30% variable, quarterly payments	Formula	Management	Proactive, in person to selected customers	Sales +10%, profit upside 15%	Immediate implementation, profit impact expected in 3 months
13. Penetrate new customer segments	Sell Product B to non-commercial customers	Target group enlarged by 50%	New target groups addressed	Sales management	Active, using target group media	Sales +10% but higher costs; profits still rise slightly	Soon after new marketing strategy developed
17. Mobilize top sales excellence	Share methods of top sellers X, Y and Z with others	Cover all salespeople	Workshops and training	Sales management	Internal only	Sales +5%, good profit growth	Implementation straight after training, impact within a month
22. Give discounts in kind, not price discounts	D comes free with a purchase of Product C (same product group)	Buy four of C, get one D free	Offer to all, entered at product group level	Product group managers	In person during sales talks	Sales +7%, slight profit growth	Sales impact immediately following communication
25. Increase prices under the customer's radar	Prices of E, H and K are little noticed; raise them	Raise prices by 8%	Price increases for all customers	Product manager	Reactive, in person	Sales - 3% but positive profit impact	Immediate implementation and impact
27. Charge separately for hitherto included services	Start charging for minor repairs	Regular hourly fee, pro rata	Case-by-case decisions	Salespeople	Reactive, in person	Revenue +2%, profits +5%	Immediate impact

Fig. 8.3: Implementation process with parallel stages

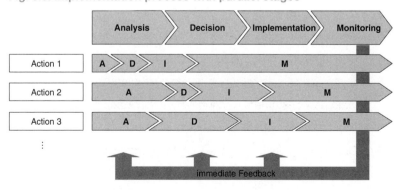

however, calls for a more detailed analysis. Once this analysis has been carried out, the decision can be made quickly. Solution 3 needs to be discussed internally at length, so the decision takes longer and the implementation follows considerably later. Feedback must be rapid in order to rectify any undesired developments.

One of the advantages of crises is that they foster the internal acceptance of unusual solutions and the speed of their implementation. "When things are going well, people resist major changes and try to get by with minor adaptations. A crisis provides the leader with the platform to get things done that were required anyway and offers the sense of urgency to accelerate their implementation," says Bill George, professor at Harvard Business School. Management must take advantage of this opportunity.[7] Many of the ideas that companies might only have dreamed about in good times can now be turned into reality – and quickly, too.

Customizing the Quick Solutions to Your Specific Situation

The 33 quick solutions in this book are intended to provide food for thought and to induce managers to fight against the crisis. The solutions should, of course, be adapted to the specific situation. Not all solutions fit each business. Vitra, a renowned manufacturer of designer furniture, including many classic items, chose to modify some of the quick solutions in line with its own challenges and goals. The ten solutions, which Vitra adopted and which focus mainly on sales activities, are shown in Figure 8.4.

Fig. 8.4: Quick solutions implemented by Vitra

1. Target stable industries and companies
2. Talk to more decision makers at trade shows and conferences
3. Organize more customer events
4. Conduct a "Phone & Coaching" team selling campaign
5. Use internal staff for telephone sales
6. Systematically activate non-active customers
7. Gain new customers with innovative trial leasing offers
8. Promotion campaign for selected classics
9. Create an ideas board for young target groups
10. Launch "boss to boss" selling

Realistically, not all of these quick solutions will have a strong and rapid impact on sales. Overall, however, Managing Director Rudolf Puetz expects them to play a significant role in beating the sales crisis. The last solution in the Vitra-program, "boss to boss"-selling, is of particular interest. During a crisis, top managers need to be more visible on the customer and the sales fronts, even if their actual sales remain symbolic. This is backed up by Siemens CEO Peter Loescher, who says, "I am the No. 1 salesperson at Siemens."[8] Remember that Siemens has over 400,000 employees and revenues of over $100 billion. When sales become a bottleneck, even the CEO needs to step in at the sales front. Fighting bottlenecks is a duty of top management.

Using Quick Methods

Although speed is of the essence, decisions should be backed up solidly from a methodological and a material point of view in order to avoid making grave errors. This is where quick methods come into play. Comprehensive, time-consuming market research studies are generally unsuitable for the quick solutions we have outlined. Some representativeness and reliability will have to be sacrificed; this is an inevitable compromise under the circumstances. We will now describe some quick methods that are suitable for the crisis.

Analyzing Available Data

In our experience, only a handful of companies actually use the information they have at their disposal. "Look at your data" was the advice offered by the well-known statistician Oscar Kempthorne.[9] Internal data should therefore be one of the first starting points for identifying and assessing potential quick solutions. Data can be analyzed in a short space of time if the company has modern data systems. The discount analyses shown in Figs. 6.5 and 6.6 illustrate what can be achieved with the help of internal data. But the possibilities extend much further, and can be applied to all sales instruments:

- Revenues, margins, costs per customer, segments, branches, regions, and so on.
- Effectiveness of advertising and promotions.
- Measuring price and discount elasticities.

- Sales according to various sales channels.
- Cross-selling and other interdependencies.

In many markets, transactions are today recorded for each individual customer. This holds true even in the retail sector, if the customer has a loyalty card or makes an online purchase. In such cases, it is possible to determine exactly how customers respond to various stimuli. This knowledge can be used for special promotions. Amazon, for example, regularly recommends books to its customers that are related to their previous purchases. The company's own data contains all of the information necessary to do this.

Surveying Experts and Customers

Expert surveys are conducted to obtain insights from experts with in-depth knowledge of markets, market reactions or customer behavior.[10] These experts can be company employees (senior executives, managers, sales representatives), management consultants, market researchers with expertise in the relevant market, retailers or customer represen-tatives. Expert surveys are recommended in cases where it would be too expensive or too time-consuming to conduct a customer survey – such as during a crisis. As expert surveys are quick and inexpensive, they are often used in conjunction with other methods. Expert surveys can take the form of unstructured interviews, or they can be structured using questionnaires, discussion guidelines or workshop formats. Unstructured surveys are helpful for generating new ideas and approaches, while the structured form makes data collection and analysis easier. Workshops are useful for gaining insights from several experts at the same time.

The following recommendations result from our vast experience in conducting expert surveys:

- The number of experts included should not be lower than five to ten. Opinions usually differ widely, especially during a crisis when the uncertainty is higher than usual. Talking to a larger number of experts makes the findings more reliable.
- The experts should hold a variety of positions and represent different hierarchy levels (including both managers and sales representatives, for example). Expert surveys should be conducted by a neutral outsider.
- The findings should be discussed in a meeting with all of the experts, who should aim to reach a consensus. This approach is preferable to simply calculating averages.

Expert surveys should be conducted in three stages. First, the participants meet to discuss the basic data and agree on the underlying assumptions. Second, the survey itself is carried out. Third, the responses should ideally be entered into a computer-supported system that analyzes and visualizes the data collected. The fact that the findings come from "internal" experts, not customers, should always be borne in mind.

During a crisis it is best if relevant knowledge can be tapped without delay. For example, a large operator of parking garages called on the services of a consultant who had considerable experience in this market. At the start of the project, the company's CEO asked the consultant what would happen if prices were increased by 10%. "You'd lose three percent of your volume," replied the consultant.[11] The higher prices were tested in a large city, and the outcome was exactly as the consultant had predicted. Obviously, knowledge of the impact of the suggested price increase already existed in the expert's head. The question of whether the parking garage operator would have dared to act solely based on the consultant's experience without conducting an empirical test shall remain unanswered here.

As we have already seen, large-scale, representative customer surveys are generally not suitable during a crisis because of the urgency involved. Customers should not be entirely neglected, however. A large transportation company might have been spared a great deal of embarrassment if it had floated its idea of charging $3.25 for each personal ticket purchase – as opposed to purchases on the Internet or from vending machines – with a random sample of customers in advance. It is always better to interview a small customer sample than to ask no customers at all how they would respond to a particular change. Such quick surveys are usually conducted by telephone and take between a few hours and a few days. Simon-Kucher & Partners regularly uses this quick method for due diligence studies, where speed is essential. It is astonishing how much one can find out by making a few dozen phone calls.

Rapid focus groups can also be used to great effect. Here, a group of customers is brought together for a discussion about the proposed quick solutions. A moderator directs this discussion to make it productive. These group discussions reveal whether the management's assumptions about customer reactions are correct. Carefully listening to the customers can help the company avoid making the serious mistakes described above. Another advantage is that expert interviews and quick customer surveys are much less expensive than representative customer studies.

Applying Trial and Error

If time and cost aspects make it impossible to reliably predict all of the consequences of implementing a certain quick solution, a rapid alternative is to conduct a small-scale test. Applying trial and error keeps the risks to a minimum. The test is carried out in a small setting such as a single store or town. One example is BMW's recent test with refurbished spare parts, which it conducted in one city and which we referred to in Chap. 7.[12] It is important to observe the outcome closely and, if necessary, to take corrective action immediately. This limits any potential damage. The parking garage operator mentioned above was concerned about possible negative reactions to the intended price increase, so it decided to test the higher prices before implementing them in just one city. After two weeks the customer response was clear – and it was benign as predicted by the consultant. Compared to surveys, the trial and error approach has the advantage that the findings reflect actual customer behavior. Not all of the 33 quick solutions are easy to test, however. For a national car rental company that advertises on television and in national newspapers, it would be difficult to conduct a regional trial of a new price structure, for example.

Postponing Irreversible Decisions

The current crisis implies extreme uncertainty. One way of tackling this is to postpone decisions that cannot be changed. During a workshop, the CEO of an automotive manufacturer said, "We're just starting to develop a follow-up model that's due to enter the market in six years' time. What will the segments look like in 2015? What long-term effects will the crisis have on the market segmentation?" At the moment there are no reliable answers to these questions. Although it might be possible to envisage alternative future scenarios, they provide only limited help for decision making. Given this insecurity the author suggested that the CEO postpone irreversible decisions for as long as possible and to leave enough scope for alternative courses of action in the future. This may only work for a limited period of time, but by then we may have a more solid view of the future.

Rapid implementation requires real-time monitoring and controlling. The nature of the crisis implies that the outcomes of the quick solutions are inevitably subject to a great deal of uncertainty and variance. This makes it all the more important to identify undesired developments as early as possible and to take quick corrective action. The effects of the quick solutions must therefore be measured as they occur, and monitored in a way that enables unwanted consequences to be discovered immediately. Peter Loescher, CEO of Siemens, explains how he does it during the crisis, "Our CFO Joe Kaeser and I now have monthly operating reviews with all of our divisions. We focus on early warning indicators so that we can see very early on what's ahead. Previously we met with our divisions only four times a year."[13]

Traffic light systems help to visualize the situation clearly. Green means everything is under control, yellow signals show ongoing observation, and red means danger. Figure 8.5 illustrates such a system. Taking into account the revenue development per customer, deviations from the revenue target, and a concluding profitability check, ongoing monitoring enables unwanted developments to be identified and rectified early on.

When an airplane flies in poor weather, the pilot needs better information systems than in good weather. Terms like "wall of fog" or "sailing in the darkness" are buzzwords of the current crisis. As with the situation of the airplane in bad conditions, these metaphors demonstrate the need for more immediate monitoring and controlling systems.[14] But even the most sophisticated data systems do not eliminate the necessity to keep a close, direct eye on the customer and the

Fig. 8.5: Traffic light system for real-time monitoring

customer ID	revenue (Mean of the last three months)	revenue development	Check 1: revenue development	same tendency within the last 12 months	revenue target	deviation from the revenue target	Check 2: target achievement	same tendency within the last 12 months	on-top discount	Check 3: profitability	effective discount
14 123 234 4	1 758	−19%	●	3	1 850	−5%	◎	10	10%	●	22%
14 365 456 5	1 520	−2%	○	6	1 500	+1%	○	2	10%	◎	19%
14 456 345 4	4 736	−40%	●	8	9 100	−48%	●	5	5%	●	36%
14 543 234 2	5 007	−15%	●	2	5 500	−9%	◎	8	0%	○	25%
14 546 454 6	6 897	−27%	●	1	8 750	−21%	●	6	10%	◎	41%
14 646 332 1	582	−8%	◎	7	550	+6%	○	3	15%	●	28%
14 654 234 2	2 276	+4%	○	3	2 500	−9%	◎	4	10%	●	46%
14 878 676 4	1 157	−14%	●	6	1 700	−32%	●	7	5%	◎	24%
14 933 534 4	3 786	−74%	●	4	6 642	−43%	●	3	0%	●	35%

○ green   ◎ yellow   ● red

market. Managers now need to talk directly to sales representatives and customers even more often than they should in good times, they need to find out what the sentiment "out there" is really like.

Training

To a large extent, the success of the quick solutions suggested in this book rests on whether the employees understand, accept and put them into daily practice. In Chapter 1 we saw how the crisis has changed customers' needs and motives (fear, risk perception, the advance of hard value and cost advantages, and so on). Account managers, salespeople, and other team members need to adapt their lines of argumentation accordingly. This calls for additional training, not only for the people who have direct customer contact, but also for in-house staff who support the sales activities. In Chapter 5 we discussed the case of a company that offered training workshops for "normal" sales representatives in order to mobilize top sales performance.

A project conducted recently for a bank offers an instructive example. During the implementation stage, consultants from Simon-Kucher & Partners offered training to more than 500 customer advisors about success factors in negotiations. Figure 8.6 outlines the key topics covered.

In times of crisis it is even more vital than usual for salespeople to emphasize the tangible benefits of their products, and to communicate these benefits effectively. At a bank, every advisor repeatedly faces customer demands for discounts on account fees, higher rates

Fig. 8.6: Example of a training program

	Objective	Action
We	1. Know, what we stand for 2. Know, where to go 3. Know, how to get there	• Be aware of the own self-concept • Define target products • Identify value driver
Customers	4. Assess customers correctly 5. Great conversation skills 6. Convince customers successfully	• Identify and respond to different customer needs • Exchange best practices • Practice, practice, practice
Competitors	7. Knowledge of the market 8. Awareness of own advantages 9. Correct reaction to competitors behavior	• Monitor competitors • Highlight competitive advantages • Guideline for argumentation

of interest on savings, or better financing terms. Choosing the right counter-arguments is crucial here. To do this, advisors have to know their customers, be well prepared, be aware of competitors' prices, and highlight the competitive advantages of their own products. This may sound trivial, but it is actually a tremendous challenge.

Raising awareness of margins, prices, price enforcement, and negotiations is extremely important. Applied correctly, it can quickly boost profits. In the case of this midsized bank, the average margin for new accounts climbed by ten base points. Assuming a financing volume of $10 billion, this corresponds to $10 million in additional profits in the first year alone.

Employing Consultants

Should consultants be involved when a company develops and assesses quick solutions, or is it better to draw on in-house expertise only? There is no standard answer to this question. If you ask a consultant (such as the author of this book), you would expect him or her to say that consultants should be involved – but the matter is not that simple.

Some companies, especially major corporations, have stopped all of their consulting projects due to the crisis, and are freezing their budgets for such projects. But others, which would normally be less likely to employ consultants, are now doing so more often because they are experiencing a workforce pinch. This is increasingly the case with midsized companies. However, many consulting projects focus too closely on cost-cutting and restructuring, while completely ignoring the opportunities on the revenue side.

What is the best course of action during the crisis? First, the decision on whether to employ consultants should be addressed objectively and not emotionally. The following questions are relevant:

- Will a consulting project result in rapid, verifiable improvements in costs, sales, revenue, price, sales efficiency, and so on? "Verifiable" should be interpreted with a good measure of common sense. Market effects can never be predicted with complete accuracy, but the robustness of the envisaged effects nevertheless differs widely. In this connection, the consultants should be required to demonstrate the quantifiable improvements they have achieved in the past.
- Equally important is the question of how quickly the effects will be experienced and how soon the project costs will be recouped. As

discussed in Chap. 2 (and Fig. 2.5 in particular), sales and price projects often have a more rapid impact and payback period than cost projects. The example of a large $100 billion corporation shows how this view is shared in practice. In a memo to the division managers, the CEO announced that consulting projects would be generally discontinued. But then he stated, "Exceptions must be approved by the CEO or the CFO. It must be demonstrated that the financial benefit of the proposed project will verifiably and considerably exceed the project costs in the current fiscal year." This appears to be a sensible attitude toward employing consultants during the crisis.

Given the seriousness of the current situation, consulting projects need to result in hard benefits. Nonessential projects are taking a back seat. The severity of the crisis means that the best available knowledge must be mobilized – and in certain areas this knowledge resides with the consultants. More and more companies have realized the necessity of involving external consultants in recent years. Drawing on experience and solutions from other industries has become especially valuable.

Speed is another crucial aspect of consulting projects. The expertise of good consultants can be harnessed immediately, as we saw in the example of the parking garage operator. What's more, experienced consultants are quick to obtain information from clients' systems and employees. An adept consultant can achieve more in a 1-day workshop than an in-house team can achieve in two weeks. Figure 8.7 shows

Fig. 8.7: Workshop about quick solutions in the crisis

9 to 9:30 am	Welcome and introductions; compare goals with participants' expectations
9:30 to 10:45 am	Identify possible quick solutions: • Customer orientation • In-house and external sales • Tender and price management • Services
10:45 to 11 am	Coffee break
11 am to 12:30 pm	Assess impact: • Sales/market share • Profits/liquidity
12:30 to 1:30 pm	Lunch break
1:30 to 4 pm	Plan the implementation of the solutions selected: • Solution 1 (structure, responsibilities, communication) • Solution 2 (structure, responsibilities, communication) • Solution 3 (structure, responsibilities, communication)
4 to 4:30 pm	Summary of findings and to-do list

an agenda for a quick solutions workshop for a company from the building technology sector.

The preparation for this workshop involved internal data analyses and meetings with managers and selected sales representatives, plus several telephone interviews with customers. At the end of the workshop a to-do list was drawn up with lines of responsibility and fixed deadlines.

Figure 8.8 outlines an immediate plan of action, made with the help of consultants, in which office staff were redeployed to the salesforce of a consumer goods company.

The company in question has 300 sales representatives. It chooses to implement quick solution 15 (Redeploy in-house staff to sales) and send 100 in-house staff to join the salesforce. These people receive brief training, shadow the sales reps for a few days, draw up a list of target customers, and then start their sales activities (in person or by telephone). Within three months the redeployed staff is expected to achieve about one third of the sales results of the regular salesforce. As the salesforce grows by 33%, this implies additional sales of about 11%. Assuming that sales would have dropped by 25% without this quick solution, the expected fall in sales is now only about 17%.[15] If achieved, this is a considerable improvement that, in conjunction with a cost-cutting program, may save the company from collapse.

Fig. 8.8: Example of a project for redeploying in-house staff to sales

To do:	100 internal staff will be redeployed to the sales force. Existing sales force of 300 staff will therefore be increased by 33%.
How?	• Training • Support sales reps • Draw up target list • Deployment to sales
Who is responsible?	Sales managers in cooperation with office managers, group leaders
Expected impact:	• Office staff achieve approx. 1/3 of sales force staff • Sales expected to drop by only 17 percent instead of 25 percent
When?	Within three months

Leadership in the Crisis

The current crisis is confronting both executives and the people they lead with an unfamiliar situation. Management guru Ram Charan considers this unfamiliarity a real problem for leaders and employees.[16] The vast majority of top managers know only what it is like to move upward. They learned their trade when times were good. They know how to manage expansion, how to enter new markets, and how to motivate employees with forward-looking targets. An American headhunter calls these managers "strategic creators."[17] Of course, there are also companies and industries that have faced decline in the past, and managers who have experienced that ought to be better prepared for the current crisis. But now that companies have to deal with slumps on all fronts, even old restructuring hands are facing new, unknown challenges. Restructuring a company when times are good is a completely different matter to doing so when the going gets really tough.

In this context we must also examine the role of the various senior executives. The CEO naturally shoulders the main responsibility for leadership and company morale. This crisis makes life especially difficult for the head of sales, because he or she is in charge of dealing with the most serious bottlenecks. There is pressure from above to sell more units, and pressure from below to enforce lower prices for the sake of the sales team. This is where the CFO comes in. It is his or her task to help stabilize prices by backing up the head of sales.

Employees start to fear for their jobs when a crisis strikes. How should this fear be addressed? What should be communicated internally, and how? What about external communication (public relations, investor relations) about the company's situation and intentions? Does the crisis call for new managers? Should the leaders send out optimistic signals or stick to the facts? How can executives maintain their credibility? There are no simple answers to these questions. Ultimately each manager must answer these questions individually. The most important aspect is to remain authentic and credible.

Summary

As noted by the U.S. banker Walter Brittain, "You can come up with the best strategy in the world. The implementation is 90 percent of its success."[18] This holds even more true in times of crisis. We summarize as follows:

- Speed of implementation gains importance during a crisis. Decisions must be made and implemented quickly.
- However, this urgency conflicts with the need to avoid making serious mistakes. The risk of an error being fatal is much greater in a crisis situation.
- The quick solutions must be chosen carefully despite the time pressure. The criteria to consider include general feasibility, speed of implementation, sales impact, costs, profit contribution, and risk. A quantitative assessment is recommended for choosing which quick solutions to adopt.
- For each quick solution it must be decided what will be done, what form the implementation will take, who will be responsible, how the solution will be communicated, and which effects will be felt when.
- The implementation process should follow the model of simultaneous engineering, where various steps take place concurrently.
- Information should be collected using quick methods such as analyzing available data, expert surveys, simplified customer surveys, and trial and error. Speed becomes more important than representativeness.
- Irreversible decisions should be postponed for as long as possible due to the extreme uncertainty.
- Outcomes should be monitored and controlled without delay in order to detect unwanted developments and take corrective action immediately.
- The decision of whether to employ consultants should be based not on cost, but on hard, verifiable improvements and a rapid payback.
- Leaders and managers face tough, unknown challenges during this crisis. Authenticity and credibility become even more important than in good times.

If a company manages to make rapid decisions, implements them quickly, and avoids making grave mistakes, it is already a large step closer to beating the crisis. Resolute implementation is the most important aspect of all.

Endnotes

1 Martin Noé, Thomas Werres, "Führen statt klagen," *Manager Magazin*, March 2009, p. 38.
2 Kotler and Caslione discuss this danger in their new book, *Chaotics*.

3 Personal discussion with Hermut Kormann, former CEO of Voith AG. Voith is an engineering conglomerate and global market leader in several fields. It was founded in 1906.

4 Hermut Kormann, "Gibt es so etwas wie typisch mittelständische Strategien?" Discussion paper No. 54, University of Leipzig, Faculty of Economics, November 2006, p. 1.

5 "Inside Obama's Economic Crusade," *Fortune*, March 9, 2009, p. 47.

6 In simultaneous engineering the various stages of the research and development process run concurrently instead of in sequence. This not only saves time and money, but also results in higher quality because development, production, procurement and marketing are coordinated from an early stage.

7 Bill George, "Seven Lessons for Leading in Crisis," wsj.com, March 15, 2009.

8 Martin Noé, Thomas Werres, "Führen statt klagen," *Manager Magazin*, March 2009, p. 38.

9 See Lance A. Waller and Carol A. Gatway, *Applied Spatial Statistics for Public Health Data*, Hoboken, New Jersey; Wiley 2004.

10 See Ludwig Berekoven, Werner Eckert and Peter Ellenrieder, *Markforschung: Methodische Grundlagen und praktische Anwendung*, Wiesbaden: Gabler 1999, and Peter Hammann and Bernd Erichson, *Marktforschung*, Stuttgart: G. Fischer 1994.

11 The implied price elasticity is therefore 0.3 (3% divided by 10%).

12 See Hermann Simon, *Preismanagement*, second edition, Wiesbaden: Gabler 1992, p. 451.

13 Martin Noé, Thomas Werres, "Führen statt klagen," *Manager Magazin* March 2009, pp. 38–43.

14 See also Hermann Simon and Martin Fassnacht, *Preismanagement*, third edition, Wiesbaden: Gabler 2009.

15 A 25% drop in sales means that sales stand at 75. If the sales performance increases by 11% due to the redeployed staff, the sales level reaches $75 \times 1.11 = 83.25$. Sales therefore drop only 16.75% (rounded up to 17%).

16 See Ram Charan, *Leadership in the Era of Economic Uncertainty*, New York: McGraw Hill 2009.

17 "Managing Along the Cutting Edge," *Newsweek*, February 9, 2009, p. 46.

18 Walter Brittain was chairman of the Bankers Trust bank, which was taken over by Deutsche Bank in the 1990s.

Chapter 9

Beyond the Crisis

Nobody can currently tell what course the crisis will take, how long it will last, or what lies beyond it. Long-term decisions have to be made, but they rest on conjecture and highly speculative scenarios. This concluding chapter should be understood against the backdrop of this extreme uncertainty. Its contents are intended to serve as food for thought – no more and no less. As we saw in Chapter 8, uncertainty about future developments means that managers should aim to achieve maximum flexibility by postponing decisions that tie their hands in the long term.

The Course of the Crisis: V, U, L or Hysteresis?

What course will the crisis take? Will it look like a V, with the abrupt drop followed by a rapid, steep recovery? Or will it be more like a U-shape with a longer period (a year or perhaps even several years) between the decline and the upturn? The V and U forms imply that there will be a return to the former levels. Far more serious would be an L-shaped development with a permanent, or at least long-lasting, backslide. Can the recession turn into a depression? More probable than the L form, however, is a hysteresis pattern in which the recovery is partial rather than complete. Hysteresis describes the persistence of an effect after its cause has vanished.[1] Magnetics offers a well-known example: When the magnetic field around an object is strengthened, the object's magnetization increases. If the magnetic field is then removed, some magnetization is left behind. This is known as remanence.

Hysteresis is frequently observed in the economy as well.[2] After a recession, for example, unemployment often does not return to pre-recession levels but stays at an intermediate level. This is called a

H. Simon, *Beat the Crisis: 33 Quick Solutions for Your Company*,
DOI 10.1007/978-1-4419-0823-0_9, © Hermann Simon 2010

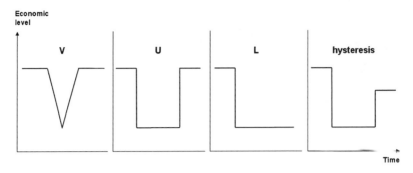

Fig. 9.1: Possible courses of the crisis

"jobless" recovery. Similar phenomena occur in foreign trade. A country's trading position can shift as a result of exchange rate adjustments, and this change often remains in place after the exchange rates have returned to their former levels. The U.S. did not completely regain its trading position following the appreciation of the dollar in the mid-1980s, even though the dollar dropped considerably in the next decade.[3] Will the current crisis be marked by such a hysteresis pattern? Figure 9.1 outlines these possible future courses of the crisis.

Nobody can answer these questions with certainty at the moment. It is, however, obvious that the course and, in particular, the duration of the crisis will have a critical impact on companies' ability to survive. Certain activities such as astute liquidity management enable a company to overcome a short-lived crisis. But if the crisis persists, and if revenues remain at a significantly lower level than before, far more radical tactics will be needed. The longer the crisis lasts, the more unlikely the V shape becomes. In the meantime it seems that the duration of the crisis is the more important aspect compared to the current size of the decline.

Companies can cope with a deep slump if it is short term, but a longer-term slump of lesser magnitude is very dangerous. Every company leader is therefore advised to think carefully about how to respond to potential long-term declines in his or her business. The CEO of a $50 billion company in the engineering sector shared his concerns with us, "Our orders are down by 40 percent in 2009. We are solidly financed and can survive this glut for nine or twelve months. But I don't know how we will respond if this lasts for two or three years. I have no idea how we can survive this situation long term." These concerns are increasingly common. The solutions are anything but evident.

When we talk of V-, U-, L- or hysteresis-shaped patterns, we are usually referring to the development of the whole economy or a specific industry. Individual companies are inevitably affected by these developments as well, but they are not entirely helpless or defenseless against them. Demonstrating that a company can detach itself to a certain degree from such unfavorable trends and providing means to tackle the situation is the purpose of this book. Even if a particular industry shrinks by 30 or 40%, a prudent company with the right sales strategy may be able to limit its revenue decline to half of this percentage. If it additionally succeeds in cutting costs by 15 or 20%, it has a good chance of survival even if the crisis persists for several years. The possibility of a long-lasting L- or hysteresis-shaped crisis makes it even more important to combine cost-cutting and revenue-boosting measures. The challenge is to survive, or ideally even to emerge from the recession stronger than before. After the Great Depression some companies really took off, General Electric is a case in point. Socio-political considerations form the framework within which a company operates. We will therefore now look at long-term consequences the crisis may have on the society and on politics.

Socio-Political Consequences of the Crisis

The socio-political framework will undergo major changes as a result of the crisis. New facts have already emerged and they will shape the future. Among them are soaring public debt, escalating money supply, growing unemployment, and the threat of protectionism.

Increasing Social Tensions

The impact of the crisis will vary by social group, country, and region. According to one economic advisor, "people with low qualifications and low incomes will be hit hardest. In good and in bad times these people are more likely than higher-qualified employees to lose their jobs. During a crisis, this imbalance becomes even more pronounced."[4] The same is true with the real estate bubble. The housing industry that was the last to benefit is the first to be hurt. This is typically the stock that is furthest out from the core of functioning cities. Foreclosure rates in low income areas in Florida are highest. Or if we take deteriorating employment conditions, those without a college degree in the rust belt (e.g., Ohio or Michigan) are most heavily affected.

Discrepancies in wealth will widen, inevitably leading to increasing social tensions. The social climate is already becoming more tense, and this will continue as unemployment rises. In a recent study, 77% of the 5,000 respondents stated that there was a sharp conflict between rich and poor, up from 55% ten years ago.[5] The crime rate is also expected to rise. In a nutshell, the crisis will make the world a more insecure place. It remains to be seen whether radical political groups will gain support as the current crisis unfolds. However, it cannot be compared with the depression of the 1930s in this respect – at least not yet.

The crisis will also have a varying regional impact. In Europe, tension has already been mounting between the Eastern and Western members of the European Union. Civil unrest has to be expected in emerging and developing countries. According to the Chinese Prime Minister Wen Jiabao, China needs "about 8 percent growth in order to prevent such disturbances."[6] Dominique Strauss-Kahn, Managing Director of the International Monetary Fund, talks of a "third wave" during which emerging economies will be destroyed and the fight against poverty will experience a setback.[7]

Growing social tensions will have a negative impact on working atmosphere and productivity. Michael Pieper, President and CEO of Franke Group, reports, "In good times we have about one theft in a factory or a warehouse per month, but now thefts have become frequent."[8] Market demand for security products and services is growing. In the U.S., sales of safes have been growing by 50% in recent months. A builder of fences reported strong growth to the author. On the other side, sales of conspicuous status symbols are expected to drop. Luxury cars sell rather poorly in countries where either conspicuous consumption is not socially accepted or where social tensions are strong. Widening social discrepancies also induce a broader spread of real estate prices and categories, ranging from poverty housing to gated communities with restricted access. It is unlikely that the crisis will lead to such extreme divergences in highly developed countries, but trends will go some way in this direction. Careful observation and appropriate precautionary measures are advised for companies.

From Deflation to Inflation

Overcapacity will continue to exert pressure on prices in the short term. Furthermore, consumers are saving more money in response to the crisis. "Banks, companies and budgets keep their additional liquidity for the time being and don't spend it. So asset prices and consumer prices are not going up," states an economic expert.[9] In many countries consumer prices have been falling in the course of 2009.[10] An American acquaintance wrote to the author, "One of the good things about the crisis is that it's easy to get cheap theater tickets in New York. And a three-course meal in a top restaurant now costs just $30 or $40." In the long term, however, we will face high inflation. This is one of the few predictions made in this book of which the author is certain. As national debts skyrocket and money supply soars, the inevitable consequence will be massive monetary devaluation. As a reaction the price of gold is likely to increase in the coming years – despite short-term fluctuations. Gold and real assets will become popular forms of investment because they offer protection against inflation.

It is hard to imagine that the government will not use rising inflation to get rid of its debts. Whether there will be a currency reform or even a return to the gold standard remains to be seen.[11] However, it is revealing that such ideas increasingly appear in public debate.[12] Henry Kissinger, for example, recently argued in favor of a new Bretton Woods system.[13] So far the author has not met anyone who can offer a plausible solution to the growing public debt. This is not a good sign.

These consequences of the crisis will present companies with new challenges. In times of deflation it is better to have low debt; in times of inflation the opposite is true. Pricing is difficult during deflation. The pressure to follow the downward price trend must be balanced against the need to postpone these cuts for as long as possible – this is not easy. When inflation sets in all this has to be changed. Under inflation companies are better off increasing prices frequently and overproportionally. Our projects in Brazil have demonstrated that consumers lose the ability to judge prices when inflation is very high. In such cases it makes little sense to offer low prices. Instead, it is better to outpace the inflation rate with price increases, and to invest more money in advertising.

More Government Regulation

One of the more dramatic consequences of the crisis will be an increase in government regulation. Since the crisis began new regulation has mainly focused on banks and insurance companies,[14] but it will not remain restricted to the financial sector. Governments are exerting influence in more and more areas. Even issues that were previously taboo, such as expropriation, are starting to appear on the agenda.[15] And governments will take greater control of management matters such as executive pay and appointments to boards. Compliance is already a heavy burden for many companies, and will become even heavier. Even core business processes are no longer safe from government intervention. Yale economist Robert Shiller argues in favor of independent financial advisors who are subsidized by the state and paid an hourly fee by the client, but receive no additional commissions. Shiller also recommends that credit insurance for consumers be made compulsory, as is the case with car insurance. There is no shortage of further ideas of this kind. In various countries we find proposals for checklists or public seal of approval for investment products.[16]

The international scope of surveillance and regulation is set to increase. Given that cases abroad fall outside the jurisdiction of national supervisory agencies, the London G20-summit in April 2009 called for an enforced international monitoring of financial markets. "No regions should remain unsupervised," one expert states. "We must put an end to regulation arbitrage."[17] Companies will have to invest more time and effort in complying with government regulations in the future.

In view of increasing national debt and social tensions, governments will place heavier financial burdens on the wealthy and on flourishing companies. Left-wing parties all over the world are demanding tax increases for high-earners. It will become more difficult for individuals and companies to avoid such tax burdens by making international arrangements. The pressure on tax havens is mounting.

Deglobalization

Globalization has been one of the strongest drivers of prosperity in recent decades. The term was coined back in 1944, but it was not until 1983 that it became more widespread due to Theodore Levitt's acclaimed article "The Globalization of Markets" in the *Harvard Business Review*.[18] Global exports per head stood at $6 in 1900; by 2008, they had climbed to $2,405 – in spite of a much larger world population. In absolute figures, global exports increased much more than a thousandfold, from $9.9 billion in 1900 to $16,127 billion in 2008.[19] These figures demonstrate how far the international division of labor has advanced. All countries profit from this development, though in varying degrees.[20] Interestingly the two biggest exporters in recent years are two very different countries with regard to the stage of their economic development – Germany and China. The U.S. is a close third in the exporters' league.

Deglobalization, or the reversal of the globalization process, poses the greatest threat in the current crisis. The economic historian Niall Ferguson of Harvard University talks of a "nightmare scenario in which history repeats itself and globalization collapses."[21] In the 1930s, the swell of protectionism that originated in the U.S. was one of the main causes of the Great Depression. The Smoot-Hawley Tariff Act, passed on June 17, 1930, imposed tariffs of up to 60% on more than 20,000 products. It was passed by Congress even though 1,028 economists had signed a petition against this legislation. Furious governments around the world retaliated with their own tariffs on U.S. goods[22] and global trade plummeted by more than 50% in the ensuing six months. The tremendous benefits of the international division of labor therefore vanished into thin air within a few months.

The danger of protectionism lies in its populist appeal. When politicians call for protectionist measures, they can be sure of mass support. American politicians are not immune to this temptation. The economic stimulus plan of early 2009 requires that iron and steel used in American infrastructure projects be produced in the United States. Although President Obama has watered down the "Buy American" provisions, a fatal chain reaction still cannot be entirely ruled out. Spain's Industry Minister Miguel Sebastián takes a similar stance, "There is something our citizens can do for their country: support Spain and its products." And President Nicolas Sarkozy of France wouldn't approve credit for French automotive manufacturers unless they promise not to outsource jobs to other countries. Thankfully, the European Union clamps down hard on national egoism of this kind. Elsewhere, the approach is more level-headed. "We need an open global economy," states German Chancellor Angela Merkel, "without a doubt, protectionism would turn the recession into a depression." Even Russian Prime Minister Vladimir Putin takes an anti-protectionist position. "We must not slide back into isolationism and economic egoism," he warns. However, such lip service by no means guarantees that defenses are not being built out of the public eye.[23] The London G20-summit of April 2009 gives reason for some optimism that at least extreme protectionism can be contained.

What do deglobalization and growing protectionism mean for the business sector? Today, many international companies are well positioned for a globalized world. Many of them run sales and manufacturing operations in foreign countries. These operations are optimally integrated into the international division of labor. If customs barriers are reinforced as a result of the crisis, this optimized division of labor could experience a major setback. On the other hand, companies with manufacturing operations abroad are already regarded as "insiders" in these countries. If protectionism increases they should actually manufacture more in the countries with high import duties cut back on cross-border deliveries. In addition, they would have to reconsider their industrial location policies. It would become necessary to open manufacturing facilities in all key countries, as many foreign companies did in Brazil in the 1960s and 1970s or as Japanese car manufacturers did in the 1980s in the U.S. Foreign manufacturing investments would therefore have to increase, at least in the most important target markets. Deglobalization should not call into question the fundamental globalization drive, but it would certainly reshape the concrete strategies for globalization. A positive side effect might be that companies would be less dependent on exchange rate fluctuations. But overall, deglobalization would have disastrous consequences for the global economy.

Worst-Case Scenarios

We cannot rule out the possibility of the current crisis turning into a nightmare scenario. "According to some estimates, the banks' losses now exceed the total equity of all banks put together," states Harvard economic historian Niall Ferguson. "In other words, the entire financial system is bankrupt."[24] Whether this is true or not, the problems facing the financial sector certainly do not appear to be solved yet. An acquaintance of the author predicts a wave of bank nationalizations in the U.S. and talks, only half-joking, of the U.S. as the "United Socialist States of America."

What might the worst-case scenario look like? The financial system collapses, protectionism spreads, unemployment surges, swathes of companies go under, deflation continues or galloping inflation emerges, public finances face ruin. It does not take much imagination to paint a worldwide horror scenario. One could inject some political ingredients to make things appear worse. The destruction of Iran's nuclear facilities (which is not unlikely in the near future) could unleash a global wave of terrorist retaliation.[25] A migration tsunami from poor to wealthy countries could take on unprecedented levels. In developing countries such as Pakistan, economic collapse might lead to the collapse of the political system and the emergence of new "Afghanistans." It is hard to imagine the actual impact of a global worst-case scenario, and even harder to advise companies on how to deal with such occurrences. But even if we do not think that these extreme scenarios are likely, we cannot completely rule them out. Fred Crawford, CEO of the restructuring firm AlixPartners, strongly urges companies to draw up emergency plans for worst-case scenarios. If revenue is expected to drop by a certain percentage, he advises having a back-up plan in case it actually falls by three times this percentage.[26] Ram Charan, one of the leading management thinkers in the U.S., expects most companies to shrink dramatically in the next two years.[27]

Market and Corporate Level: The Crisis as Catharsis

Moving from the societal to the corporate level, certain developments are already emerging. Could the crisis bring about catharsis? Aristotle described catharsis as a form of radical cleansing. A catharsis effects "misery" and "shudder" – words that resonate with the crisis – and results in being purged from dispensable exaggerations. We definitely expect that the crisis will bring about this kind of purge. Many companies will not survive the crisis, including those that in times of prosperity were marginally profitable and those that are overleveraged.

Deleveraging: Equity Reigns

The crisis will be merciless on companies with low equity ratios. Times are tough for firms that do not have this risk buffer and that are burdened by high debt, that is, are too strongly leveraged. What's more, the risks associated with large debts will increase when interest rates start rising due to inflation. Deleveraging is therefore vital. A leading investment expert urges companies to strengthen their equity base as quickly as possible.[28] His rationale is that creditworthiness suffers as operating profit falls, thereby endangering credit ratings in the future. As a result, investors might release only a limited amount of equity, or impose more restrictive conditions. Equity is set to gain importance in the coming years. As credit becomes increasingly scarce, more equity will be needed to plug the gaps – with the corresponding risks and rewards.

This will ultimately mean a return to normality, a state that has been strongly distorted in recent years.

Streamlining Product Lines

The catharsis will result in a purge of marginal and dispensable products. In a market economy it is the consumers who decide which products are necessary, but during a crisis their decision criteria can shift. Whether this change is temporary or permanent makes no difference to a company that is fighting for survival. If demand plummets or disappears for a period of time (U-, L- or hysteresis-pattern), the suppliers of marginal products will be brought to their knees. The effects are already being experienced in the media sector. If one thinks about how many magazines a well-stocked newsstand sells, one might wonder who actually buys them all.[29] In the U.S. we have already seen well-known newspapers disappearing and media companies filing for Chapter 11. The number of newspapers and magazines will drop further and significantly. In this industry, however, the crisis is not the only culprit. With the advance of the Internet, advertising spending patterns have shifted. Online advertising is expected to continue growing by 10% in 2009; in the first quarter of the year even an above-average growth of 16% was announced, while the print media will post dramatic declines in advertising revenues.[30]

Reestablishing the Balance

An important and necessary function of a crisis is to realign supply and demand in the market. The current crisis will contribute to this rebalancing. The case of the automotive industry illustrates how dramatic global imbalances have become. The global annual manufacturing capacity for automobiles stands currently at 90 million units. In 2008 about 55 million cars were actually sold. In 2009, estimates for car sales vary between 46 and 50 million. Thus, there is an overcapacity of well over 50%. This disparity becomes untenable in the long term. Without government intervention the market would align such imbalances between supply and demand by means of a crisis. But in the case of the automotive industry government intervention and protectionism are likely to postpone the necessary capacity adjustments indefinitely – to the detriment of profitable car manufacturers and the taxpayer. In other industries the government will be less interventionist, and supply and demand will be brought into line relatively quickly. This alignment will involve both the collapse of weak competitors and capacity reductions at many companies. If demand remains low for an extended period of time, the alignment process will be extremely painful.

Restructuring of Industries

New structures will emerge in many industries as a result of the crisis, and the changes will be rapid and radical. Company structures are likely to shift more in the next three years than they have in the last 20. This will certainly be the case in banking, insurance, and the automotive assembly and supply industries. The list of leading banks did not change significantly between 1987 and 2007, but since then it has been transformed – and further surprises are probably in store. American International Group (AIG), the world's largest insurance company, is today a mere shadow of its former self. Right up to 2007, General Motors was the world's leading automaker in terms of revenue and units. And many other industries that are not so much in the public eye are in for a rollercoaster ride as well. For instance, law firms that have been focusing on M&A could be in for a rough time. Which airlines will survive the crisis as independent companies? Which engineering companies will go bankrupt, be taken over or merged? How will the telecommunications industry look in five years' time? Nobody knows the answers today. But we can state with a high certainty that the structures in many sectors will change radically. There will be a few winners and probably many losers in this transition.

Merger and Acquisition Opportunities

The crisis will open up excellent merger and acquisition opportunities for companies with financial power. Prices for companies will drop to unprecedented levels, and enforced sell-offs will lead to massive undervaluation. Many companies' share prices have already plummeted to below their book value, so if the book values are not simply plucked out of the air, bargain prices are already commonplace today.

However, buyers must be aware that low prices harbor higher risks. Acquisitions during a crisis are by no means less risky than in prosperous times, no matter how cheap they are. The problem is that nobody knows exactly how the crisis will progress after the acquisition has been finalized. The acquired company can still go bankrupt if the crisis lasts longer than expected. A case in point is a prefabricated-house manufacturer, which was bought by a private equity investor at an attractive price and went into bankruptcy soon afterwards. An acquisition can throw the buyer's financing into disorder, making follow-up investments necessary. No due diligence, no matter how carefully conducted, can guarantee absolute security in times of crisis. Acquisitions must therefore be approached with great caution, however inexpensive they might seem. Many banks who took over struggling competitors in the wake of the fall of Lehman Brothers would today be happy had they observed this lesson.

Shifts in Market Segments

Segmentation in many markets is likely to shift due to the crisis. Some observers predict that the upper price segments will shrink, as we are already witnessing in the automotive industry. But will this be a permanent change? Or will we see a return to normality? Or will there be a partial recovery in the form of hysteresis? We must approach these questions with great care and level-headedness. The crisis is unlikely to fundamentally change basic human needs. Neither do we share the widespread predictions of gloom for the luxury goods market.[31] Of course, this does not mean that the upper price segments will face fewer dangers. There are marginal suppliers here too, and the first bankruptcies of luxury goods companies have already been filed.[32]

Emergence of an Ultra-Low Price Segment

The crisis may foster the emergence of a new ultra-low price segment. Signs of this development can already be seen in Eastern Europe and in Asia. The French car manufacturer Renault has been very successful with its Dacia Logan, a car produced in Rumania with a selling price of less than $10,000.[33] The average price of a Volkswagen Golf, the most popular car in Europe, is about two-and-half times as high. In emerging countries, ultra-low-priced cars are offered at much cheaper prices. Tata launched its Nano microcar in India in the spring of 2009 at a price of about $2,000.[34] The ultra-low price car segment is posting double the growth rates of the auto industry as a whole. Automotive manufacturers and suppliers will ignore this emerging segment at their peril. Bosch, the world's largest automotive supplier, developed a radically simplified, extremely inexpensive common rail technology for the Nano in India and gets more than 10% share of the car's value. Eight other suppliers from Germany are also on board, illustrating that companies from highly industrialized countries can and must keep pace in the ultra-low price segment. However, the challenge to make money there remains.

Products at ultra-low prices are emerging in other industries, too. The idea of a laptop for $100, put forward by MIT professor Nicholas Negroponte, has gained worldwide attention. A reasonable laptop can now be bought for $300, and even industry leaders such as Intel and Microsoft are entering the ultra-low price segment. Volumes in this segment will run to hundreds of millions if not billions, as illustrated by the three billion-plus cell phones in the world today. Hyundai Mobile from Korea recently demonstrated a phone that costs just over $20, which could pave the way for further market expansion.[35] According to the futurist Ray Kurzweil, the advance of nanotechnology in industries such as pharmaceuticals, biotechnology, medical technology, and mechatronics will lead to dramatic drops in costs and prices.[36] What we regard as the ultra-low price segment today could become the price standard in just a few years. It is striking that Nestlé, the world's largest food company, has announced plans to introduce low-price products for low-income consumers.[37] In the same way, the French food group Danone has created a line of low-cost yogurts in Europe that comes in smaller tubs and fewer flavors than its standard products.[38] Another novel approach is being taken by GlaxoSmithKline, the world's second-largest pharmaceutical manufacturer, which has cut some drug prices in the 50 poorest countries to a quarter of the price level in the industrial nations.[39]

Ultra-low prices are by no means restricted to consumer goods; they are also making inroads into industrial commodity markets. Siemens, for instance, aims to achieve disproportionately strong growth in emerging markets by offering more products in the low-price segment.[40] And according to a study conducted by the German Engineering Federation, "Machine and plant manufacturers need to radically simplify their product concepts to conquer growth markets such as China and India."[41]

One interesting question is whether products with ultra-low prices will advance from the emerging markets into the high-income countries. The crisis makes this more likely, as the success of the Dacia Logan illustrates. A recent study reveals that the percentage of "households that can afford almost nothing" climbed to 27% in 2008 from 19% in 2002.[42] The acceptance of innovations that deliver a sufficient performance at extremely low costs and prices will increase as a result of the crisis. Interestingly, Tata plans to build a version of the Nano that complies with American and European exhaust and safety standards.

Another question is whether a new ultra-low price segment can emerge from within. Will discount retailers such as Wal-Mart in the U.S. or Aldi and Lidl in Germany respond to the crisis by extending the price ladder downward? We cannot rule out this possibility. It appears that the price and advertising competition between aggressive discounters is heating up in the course of the crisis. Is this just another normal battle? Or are discounters aiming to capture the lead in the emerging ultra-low price segment? If so, the consequences for suppliers and higher-priced retailers would be severe.

A New Age of Modesty

Does the crisis herald a new age of modesty? "We will set our sights lower once the recession is over, and we will have to prepare for lower growth rates than before," predicts an economic expert.[43] The boom years offered numerous examples of excesses and overindulgence, such as the construction boom in Dubai and the unabashed consumerism among the nouveau riche in emerging and in developed countries. Such excesses will be leveled out as a result of the crisis.

An interesting phenomenon can be observed in the U.K., where wartime self-help books are being reprinted and experiencing a new popularity. In Germany, demand for arable land is increasing. Self-sufficiency, stockpiling, and self-restraint are becoming buzzwords once again. Is this panic or will it turn out to be prudent behavior? Is a new sense of moderation and frugality emerging? And if so, how long will it last? We are often told that five years is the usual period when it comes to internalizing and adapting to the lessons learned during a crisis. The author advises companies to be prepared for a new age of restraint that could shape consumer behavior for an extended period of time.

Despite the upheaval, we must be careful not to throw the baby out with the bathwater. People tend to exaggerate in extreme situations.

At the turn of the millennium, the euphoria surrounding the Internet age and the new economy led many observers to question the validity of fundamental economic laws. The old economy was declared dead, and those who did not agree were labeled old-fashioned and no longer taken seriously. But just a few years later, it was evident that the old-economy laws still held true, and that the new economy-skeptics had been right not to dismiss them. We are likely to see something similar with the current crisis. It will not single-handedly do away with basic human needs such as the pursuit of prestige and status. No matter how serious or long-lasting this crisis becomes, demand for luxury goods will survive. It is, however, likely that values relating to environmental awareness and energy consciousness, for example, will shift permanently. And perhaps the above-mentioned sense of moderation will gain momentum, at least for some time. Carlos Ghosn, CEO of Renault-Nissan, envisages such effects. He says, "Even after the crisis customers will attach greater importance to low costs and enhanced environmental compatibility."[44]

For entrepreneurs and managers it is crucial to understand these and other consequences of the crisis, and to draw the right strategic conclusions. In relation to all quick solutions, companies must be careful not to set the wrong course for the long term.

Summary

The long-term effects of the crisis will be no less significant than the short-term predicament. This book is primarily concerned with quick solutions that have a rapid impact. When deciding which solutions to adopt, companies need to consider their longer-term consequences. These are extremely difficult to predict. However, answering certain questions can generate valuable insights and prevent serious mistakes. Here are the key points:

- The crisis can follow a V-, U-, L-, or hysteresis pattern. The longer it continues, the more unfavorable the course is likely to become. The duration of the crisis is more critical for survival than its current extent.
- If the L-shaped or the hysteresis form takes effect, the necessary changes will be much more radical than the quick solutions described in this book.
- Social tensions are likely to rise. Companies should prepare for this, both internally and in terms of their market offerings.

- Short-term deflationary tendencies will be followed by high inflation in the long term. Pricing policy must be adapted accordingly.
- The crisis will lead to more government regulation and higher taxes.
- Deglobalization resulting from protectionism poses the greatest danger for the international division of labor and global prosperity. If this occurs, globally operating companies will have to deepen their value chain within each customs zone. This will sacrifice many of the benefits of the international division of labor.
- A worst-case scenario with very high unemployment, waves of bankruptcies, galloping inflation, and national insolvencies cannot be ruled out.
- In many markets, the crisis will result in a "purge" at the corporate level. Many companies will not survive.
- To protect themselves effectively, companies are advised to deleverage, that is, strengthen their equity base, early on. Credit is scarce and could become scarcer, and equity will become increasingly important.
- Product lines will be streamlined. Marginal and dispensable products will be edged out.
- In sectors ruled by market forces, overcapacities will be reduced and supply and demand will be brought into line. Imbalances will remain in sectors where governments intervene.
- Many industries will experience a radical restructuring as a result of the crisis. Financially strong companies will be able to acquire competitors at low prices. Such acquisitions carry high risks, however.
- Market segments will shift, with a tendency toward lower price levels. Nevertheless, the luxury and premium segments are not expected to vanish.
- A new ultra-low price segment is likely to grow strongly in emerging countries. This segment may move into highly developed nations. The longer the crisis lasts, the more likely this segment is to emerge.
- The crisis will not invalidate basic economic laws. However, the emergence of a new sense of restraint over a longer period cannot be ruled out.

The current crisis represents a completely new experience for today's generation. Only a handful of people alive today can still remember the Great Depression of the 1930s. "The mass unemployment of the 1930s shaped the destiny of an enormous collective," states the Austrian author Franz Schuh. "Those who survived were changed by the crisis for the rest of their lives."[45] In most advanced countries, the post-war generation, to which the author of this book belongs, has experienced only peace, growth, and prosperity. Never before have we been confronted with a crisis of such proportions. For the first time in our lives, we, the children of the post-war period, are challenged to fight with all our energies against a secular crisis. This book shall provide companies, managers, and their employees with the means to beat this crisis. Implementing the 33 quick solutions with determination and stamina will not undo the crisis, but it will certainly contain the damage. And this can make all the difference between a company's death and its survival.

Endnotes

1 "Hysteresis" is derived from the Greek for "to lag behind." The term was introduced to the natural sciences by the physicist J.A. Ewing in 1881.
2 "Buckle down," Economist.com, April 16, 2009
3 See also Hermann Simon, "Hysteresis in Marketing – A New Phenomenon," *MIT Sloan Management Review*, spring 1997, pp. 39–49.
4 "Gut gemeint, schlecht gemacht," *Wirtschaftswoche*, February 9, 2009, pp. 24–25.
5 "Die gefühlte Ungerechtigkeit wächst," *Frankfurter Allgemeine Zeitung*, February 10, 2009, p. 11.
6 "China stemmt sich gegen die Krise," Die Zeit online, February 2, 2009.
7 "Die dritte Welle," *General-Anzeiger Bonn*, March 4, 2009, p. 6.
8 "Kampf der Krise," *Bilanz*, February 2009, pp. 24–34.
9 "Ein Gesamtkonzept für die Rettung der Banken fehlt," *Frankfurter Allgemeine Zeitung*, February 9, 2009, p. 15.
10 "Buckle down," Economist.com, April 16, 2009
11 See Nathan Lewis, *Gold: The Once and Future Money*, Hoboken, New Jersey: Wiley 2007.
12 "Währungsreform als radikalste Folge," *General-Anzeiger Bonn*, March 7, 2009, p. 9.
13 "Change: Priorities for U.S. Politics Under the New President," speech by Henry Kissenger at the Sal. Oppenheim investors' conference, Cologne, March 9, 2009.
14 "Lessons from a crisis," Economist.com, November 19, 2008.
15 See Otto Graf Lambsdorff, "Enteignung: Nicht Ultima Ratio, sondern Offenbarungseid," *Frankfurter Allgemeine Zeitung*, March 4, 2009, p. 12.
16 "Aigner gegen einen Finanz-TÜV," *Frankfurter Allgemeine Zeitung*, March 11, 2009, p. 19.
17 Jochen Sanio, "Was ist für die Finanzaufsicht erforderlich?," speech, Club La Redoute, Bonn, March 2, 2009.
18 Thedore Levitt, "The Globalization of Markets," *Harvard Business Review*, May–June 1983, pp. 92–102.
19 Hermann Simon, *Hidden Champions des 21. Jahrhunderts*, Frankfurt: Campus 2007, p. 127 and WTO Statistics.

20 The two biggest profiteers of globalization are China and Germany, China in consumer goods, Germany in industrial goods, cf. Luis Miotti und Frédérique Sachwald, Commerce mondial: Le retour de la "vieille économie?", Paris: Institut Français des Rélations International 2006.

21 "Wir erleben die finanziellen Symptome eines Weltkrieges," Interview with Niall Ferguson, *Frankfurter Allgemeine Zeitung*, February 24, 2009, p. 12.

22 Nathan Lewis, *Gold: The Once and Future Money*, Hoboken, New Jersey: Wiley 2007, p. 226.

23 "Auge um Auge," *Wirtschaftswoche*, February 9, 2009, pp. 32–33.

24 "Wir erleben die finanziellen Symptome eines Weltkrieges," *Frankfurter Allgemeine Zeitung*, February 24, 2009, p. 12.

25 Henry Kissinger did not rule out this possibility in his speech "Change: Priorities for U.S. Politics Under the New President" at the Sal. Oppenheim investors' conference, March 9, 2009.

26 "Managing along the Cutting Edge," *Newsweek*, February 9, 2009, p. 46.

27 Ram Charan, *Leadership in the Era of Economic Uncertainty*, New York: McGraw Hill 2009.

28 Stephan Leithner, Deutsche Bank's head of German investment banking, in: "Die Qualität der Krise darf nicht unterschätzt werden," *Frankfurter Allgemeine Zeitung*, February 28, 2009, p. 21.

29 A large newsstand stocks up to 3,000 newspapers and magazines. See "Nur die Massenblätter sollen ins Regal," *Frankfurter Allgemeine Zeitung*, March 25, 2009, p. 37.

30 "Online-Werbung wächst 2009 um 10 Prozent," *Frankfurter Allgemeine Zeitung*, March 4, 2009, p. 17. and http://www.presseportal.de, "Online-Werbemarkt spürt erste Folgen der Wirtschaftskrise," April 14, 2009.

31 "Der Luxusmarkt hat seinen Glanz verloren," *Frankfurter Allgemeine Zeitung*, February 24, 2009, p. 20.

32 Examples include the Geneva-based watch manufacturer Villemont and the Italian fashion house Ittierre.

33 The selling price starts at $9,360 for the cheapest variant of the Dacia Logan.

34 The Nano is referred to in India as the "one lakh car." A lakh means 100,000. The Nano's price threshold is 100,000 rupees, or roughly US $2,000. See "Tata baut ab März sein Billigauto," *Handelsblatt*, February 26, 2009, p. 4.

35 "Hyundai Mobile: Mit Billighandys gegen die Krise," derstandard.at, February 17, 2009.

36 Ray Kurzweil, *The Singularity Is Near*, New York: Penguin Books 2005.

37 "Nestlé setzt auf billige Produkte," *General-Anzeiger Bonn*, February 20, 2009, p. 7.

38 "From Buy, Buy, to Bye-Bye," Economist.com, April 02, 2009

39 "Billigere Medikamente für arme Länder," *Frankfurter Allgemeine Zeitung*, February 16, 2009, p. 14.

40 "Siemens will Geschäft in Low-End-Märkten stärken," FAZ.net, February 20, 2009.

41 *VDI-Nachrichten*, March 30, 2007, p. 19.

42 Michael Reidel, "Rezepte in der Rezession," *Horizont*, March 5, 2009, p. 4.

43 Christoph Schmidt from the German Council of Economic Experts in: "Kleinere Brötchen," *Wirtschaftswoche*, February 9, 2009, p. 19.
44 "Renault bläst zum Rückzug," *Frankfurter Allgemeine Zeitung*, February 13, 2009, p. 18.
45 Franz Schuh, "Jetzt endet das Glück der kleinen Leute," *Frankfurter Allgemeine Zeitung*, March 3, 2009, p. 31.

Acknowledgments

First of all, I thank my wife Cecilia for suggesting I write this book. Many thanks go to Peter Fuchs, Sandra Hoffmann, Dr. Gunnar Markert, and Dorothea Hayer, the project team at Simon-Kucher & Partners. Without them it would not have been possible to complete the manuscript so quickly. I also extend my gratitude to Maureen Cueppers, Jennifer Hoehr, Ingo Lier, and Frank Luby for their hard work in meeting the translation deadline. Suggestions and examples were submitted by the following partners from Simon-Kucher & Partners: Kai Bandilla, Frank Bilstein, Dr. Fabian Braun, Dr. Gunnar Clausen, Andrew Conrad, Peter Ehrhardt, Dr. Jan Engelke, Dr. Andreas von der Gathen, Dr. Philip Grothe, Stefan Herr, Dr. Klaus Hilleke, Dr. Markus Hofer, Matt Johnson, Jörg Krütten, Dieter Lauszus, Frank Luby, Dr. Andrea Maessen, Dr. Rainer Meckes, Steve Rosen, Dr. Dirk Schmidt-Gallas, Dr. Gerald Schnell, Dr. Karl-Heinz Sebastian, Dr. Georg Tacke, Andre Weber, and Dr. Georg Wuebker. I am also indebted to the consultants Dr. Philipp Biermann, Richard Finke, Dr. Martin Gehring, Jason Gelbort, Josh Gold, Peter Harms, Olaf Hermes, Sebastian Hock, Guy Krug, Ben Micheel, Peter Schmich, Patrick J. Simon, David Vidal, and Jocelyn Whittenburg for their valuable contributions. My thanks go to Anita Mueller and Maureen Cueppers for their support with press relations. Many thanks are also due to Nicholas Philipson from Springer, New York, for his commitment and fine-tuning of the manuscript, and to Elizabeth Doyle-Aseritis for copyediting. Last but not least, I wish to thank the many entrepreneurs and managers all over the world who have spent time talking with me since the crisis began and provided invaluable insights. They have all taught me a great deal, and my intention with this book is to give back to them some of what I have learned. I hope that the tremendous speed of the work on this book has not led to an increase in errors. The responsibility for any remaining errors is mine alone.

Index